AF589153

Odes & Nightingales

Words on Nature for Every Day of the Year

A NATURE-LOVER'S LEXICON

First published in Great Britain in 2026 by Gaia, an imprint of Octopus Publishing Group Ltd
Carmelite House
50 Victoria Embankment
London EC4Y 0DZ
www.octopusbooks.co.uk

An Hachette UK Company
www.hachette.co.uk

The authorized representative in the EEA is Hachette Ireland, 8 Castlecourt Centre, Dublin 15, D15 XTP3, Ireland
(email: info@hbgi.ie)

Distributed in the US by
Hachette Book Group
1290 Avenue of the Americas,
4th and 5th Floors
New York, NY 10104

Distributed in Canada by
Canadian Manda Group
664 Annette St., Toronto,
Ontario, Canada M6S 2C8

ISBN: 978-1-7884-0680-2
eISBN: 978-1-7884-0687-1

A CIP catalogue record for this book is available from the British Library.

Printed and bound in Great Britain.

10 9 8 7 6 5 4 3 2 1

Publisher: Lucy Pessell
Compiling Editor: Robert Tuesley Anderson
Senior Editor: Katie Button
Senior Designer: Alicia House
Assistant Editor: Samina Rahman
Production Controller: Sarah Parry

This FSC® label means that materials used for the product have been responsibly sourced.

Publisher's note:
The asterisk symbol is used in the text to denote where the word derivation is theorized or reconstructed by linguists from non-textual sources.

Contents

Introduction

Odes & Nightingales
Words on Nature for Every Day of the Year

A NATURE-LOVER'S LEXICON

ROBERT TUESLEY ANDERSON

Gaia

If you've ever stepped outside after a summer rain shower and been met by the sweet fresh smell of the earth, or gazed up at swooping cloud of starlings as they wheel overhead, creating an ever-changing pattern in the evening sky, or felt your boot break through the fresh crunch of newly-fallen snow you'll know that nature has a beauty that's hard to express. And yet we are all driven to find the words to communicate our experiences. *Odes & Nightingales* is a nature-lover's lexicon: a treasure trove of words old and new – lost, imagined and rediscovered – enabling you to find the perfect word to describe an ecstatic moment.

Nature is a language that has spoken to poets, artists and writers through the ages and in these pages there are poems and passages from literature that celebrate all that the natural world has to offer. Take a journey through the seasons, and discover the beauty of our favourite words for nature: from the daffodil, the tyger and the nightingale, to the yaffingale, the dumbledore and the polliwog. You will travel to Japan for some forest *shinrin-yoku*, crunch through Inuit *katiksugnik* snow that's light and deep enough for walking and take an Icelandic summer *sólarfrí*.

From the observing the ecstatic aerial manoeuvres of a falcon, to celebrating the halcyon days of summer – whether the landscape is lit by wolflight or noonbeams: discover the beauty of evocative, descriptive or onomatopoeic words – one for every day of the year.

January

January brings the snow,
Makes our feet and fingers glow.

– 'The Months', Sara Coleridge

Picture January and it may be something straight out of a painting: snowbound fields, frost-capped hedgerows and an ice-covered pond criss-crossed by skaters – a scene to make our feet and fingers glow according to Sara Coleridge, daughter of poet Samuel Taylor Coleridge. But the reality is that this month – especially in our warming world – is more likely to be grey, drab and teeth-chatteringly cold, with not a snowflake in sight. No wonder January can be such a difficult month to negotiate – for us humans and, of course, for animals, too.

That said, January has its own beauties – pay attention and you will notice that there is plenty of animal activity going on: from a hare padding across a furrowed field, to a thrush singing its heart out in woodland, right down to species of moths and insects that are adapted to the winter climate. We need to open ourselves, like the witch Serafina Pekkala in Philip Pullman's *Northern Lights* (see 17 January), to winter's strange and magical wonders. Put those parkas on and go out to make more footprints in that snow.

darkling

I leant upon a coppice gate
  When Frost was spectre-grey,
And Winter's dregs made desolate
  The weakening eye of day.
The tangled bine-stems scored the sky
  Like strings of broken lyres,
And all mankind that haunted nigh
  Had sought their household fires.

The land's sharp features seemed to be
  The Century's corpse outleant,
His crypt the cloudy canopy,
  The wind his death-lament.
The ancient pulse of germ and birth
  Was shrunken hard and dry,
And every spirit upon earth
  Seemed fervourless as I.

At once a voice arose among
  The bleak twigs overhead
In a full-hearted evensong
  Of joy illimited;
An aged thrush, frail, gaunt and small,
  In blast-beruffled plume,
Had chosen thus to fling his soul
  Upon the growing gloom.

So little cause for carolings
  Of such ecstatic sound
Was written on terrestrial things
  Afar or nigh around,
That I could think there trembled through
  His happy good-night air
Some blessed Hope, whereof he knew
  And I was unaware.

Thomas Hardy wrote 'The Darkling Thrush' to mark the end of the 19th century and the beginning of the new one, finding hope amid the darkling – or growing darkness – of the social upheaval and polluting industrialization that had come to dominate the Victorian age. As a symbol of resilience, he choose the song thrush (*Turdus philomelos*), whose song of 'joy illimited' resounds through the wintry evening air.

2 JANUARY

chrysanthemum

Chrysanthemum bloom late, from late summer through to mid-January, and are the quintessential winter flower for Japanese poets. Here is a poem by the 9th-century Japanese writer Ōshikōchi no Mitsune lamenting the difficulty of picking the bloom in the snow:

> It was a white chrysanthemum
> I came to take away;
> But, which are coloured, which are white,
> I'm half afraid to say,
> So thick the frost to-day!

3 January — blizzard

> Worried gusts of wind were rushing to and fro over the ice and whispering in the wood by the shore. The dark-blue wall rose higher, and the gusts became stronger. Suddenly it was as if a great door had blown wide open, the darkness yawned, and everything was filled with wet, flying snow. This time it didn't come from above, it darted along the ground. It was howling and shoving like a living thing.

In Tove Jansson's *Moominland in Midwinter*, the young Moomin Moomintroll wakes up unexpectedly during the Moomin hibernation and discovers for the first time a wonderful and frightening world of snow and ice. In this beautiful yet unnerving passage, we see a blizzard from Moomintroll's point of view, as he stands awestruck and terrified by this powerful winter phenomenon.

Old as the word sounds, 'blizzard' – in the sense of snowstorm – emerged only in the late 19th century, in the United States.

4 January — ninguid

Some words exist only in the dictionary or even just in the minds of their glossophiliac compilers (there are examples in this book). Ninguid is one of these, defined by Thomas Blount in 1656 in his *Glossographia*; or, *A dictionary interpreting the hard words of whatsoever language, now used in our refined English tongue* as 'covered in snow'. The *Glossographia* included some 11,000 words, a large number of them new coinages that quickly – and quite rightly – died a death. Words need speech, just as humans need air.

algid

Late lies the wintry sun a-bed,
A frosty, fiery sleepy-head;
Blinks but an hour or two; and then,
A blood-red orange, sets again.

Before the stars have left the skies,
At morning in the dark I rise;
And shivering in my nakedness,
By the cold candle, bathe and dress.

– Robert Louis Stevenson, 'Winter-Time'

Winter days are short and invite us to stay in bed and put off the inevitable shock of facing the cold of the day.

Algid – from the Latin *algidus*, intensely cold – is most often used as a medical term for having a cold, clammy skin when suffering from malaria, but is occasionally (well, probably never) used more generally for cold, wintry conditions. The word does strike a chilly sound.

whiteout

> Yes, the newspapers were right: snow was general all over Ireland. It was falling softly upon the Bog of Allen and, further westwards, softly falling into the dark mutinous Shannon waves. It was falling too upon every part of the lonely churchyard where Michael Furey lay buried. It lay thickly drifted on the crooked crosses and headstones, on the spears of the little gate, on the barren thorns. His soul swooned slowly as he heard the snow falling faintly through the universe and faintly falling, like the descent of their last end, upon all the living and the dead.

These are the famous final lines of James Joyce's short story 'The Dead' from *The Dubliners*, about a group of family and friends attending a dinner to celebrate the Christian feast of the Epiphany. The dinner certainly proves to be a moment of epiphany – revelation – for many of those present, including the academic Gabriel Conway, whose wife reveals her girlhood love for a young man, Michael Furey, awakening in him a sense of, and compassion for, her inner life.

The term 'whiteout' for a heavy widespread snowfall is un-Joycean, of course – it was first used in the 1930s or 1940s.

7 January **purga**

> A snowstorm has been raging since early morning, crying, moaning, howling on the dismal streets of Moscow – the branches of the trees under my windows are intertwined and twisted like sinners in hell, through this noise the sad ringing of bells can be heard...What weather! What a country!

Let's head for Russia for a moment to see whether winter is any better there – in that assumedly winter-loving country of sleighs, muffs and samovars. Apparently not, if this letter from 19th-century novelist Ivan Turgenev, is anything to go by. Nonetheless, Russian has lots of words for a snowstorm, including *purga*, a fierce kind of blizzard in northern Russian (perhaps the kind described by Turgenev), and *buran*, a freezing, destructive snowstorm in Siberia.

8 January **snow-broth**

> A man, whose blood
> Is very snow-broth, one who never feels.

Shakespeare uses this term in *Measure for Measure* to describe the unfeeling villain of the piece, Angelo. Meaning cold slushy water, it is not – surprisingly – the Bard's own coinage, although it was but a very recent one.

ululate

When icicles hang by the wall,
And Dick the shepherd blows his nail,
And Tom bears logs into the hall,
And milk comes frozen home in pail;
When blood is nipped, and ways be foul,
Then nightly sings the staring owl,
'Tu-whit; Tu-whoo!' –
A merry note,
While greasy Joan doth keel the pot.

When all aloud the wind doth blow,
And coughing drowns the parson's saw,
And birds sit brooding in the snow,
And Marian's nose looks red and raw,
When roasted crabs hiss in the bowl,
Then nightly sings the staring owl,
'Tu-whit, Tu-whoo!' –
A merry note,
While greasy Joan doth keel the pot.

Some more Shakespeare, this time the cheery winter's song that ends the comedy *Love's Labour's Lost*. It is good to find for once that the owl is not as a harbinger of doom, but a merry accompaniment to human doings, even if it is the drudgery of winter tasks. The word 'owl', like its Germanic cognates such as the German *Eule*, imitates the bird's cry, related to both 'howl' and 'ululate', the latter originally meaning 'to shriek like an owl' (*ulula* is Latin for a screech owl).

10 January

chionophiles

Animals or plants that thrive in cold conditions, such as in the Arctic or alpine mountains – examples include the ptarmigan, Arctic hare and caribou. *Chios* is the Greek work for snow.

11 January

psychrophiles

These are organisms such as bacteria, algae and lichens that can survive in cold conditions. *Psukhrós* is the Greek word for cold.

12 January

firn

In glaciology, old snow that has melted once, but is not yet glacial ice.

13 JANUARY

frost-fettered

To-day I may not quit my home;
For maiden's love or maiden's plight
I dare not o'er my threshold roam;
For field and flood and vale and height
Are chained with frost, with snows are white!
Close as the scales on dragon's breast,
Those flakes would cluster round my vest;
And in a miller's lowly guise,
Conceal the bard from beauty's eyes!
Brightly to all created things
The lime-white vest of winter clings;
Fair as a grey stoled hermit's robe
It wraps this dark and dreary globe!
O'er every wood, o'er every grove,
Its veil of dazzling light is wove;
Spotless and glittering as mail,
Those snowy showers at random sail...

A translation of the first half of the great 14th-century Welsh bard Dafydd ap Gwilym's poem 'The Snow'. The notion of 'frost-fettered' is found widely in medieval poetry, suggesting how much winter's heavy snows could hamper ordinary life – whether work, play or love. Here the poet finds beauty in winter, too.

14 JANUARY

kramsnö

A word from the Finnish language for the kind of soft but firm snow that's great for making snowballs.

15 January — boreal

The night is darkening round me,
The wild winds coldly blow;
But a tyrant spell has bound me
And I cannot, cannot go.

The giant trees are bending
Their bare boughs weighed with snow.
And the storm is fast descending,
And yet I cannot go.

Clouds beyond clouds above me,
Wastes beyond wastes below;
But nothing drear can move me;
I will not, cannot go.

Emily Brontë's work moils with the harsh, wild winds of the Yorkshire Moors where she grew up, whether in her novel *Wuthering Heights* or this poem, sometimes known as 'Spellbound'.

In ancient Greece, the god of the cold north wind (and, indeed, of winter) was Boreas, usually depicted as a strong, older male with a shaggy, hoary beard. From him comes the word 'boreal', meaning northern, most often used to describe the icy, forested subarctic zone otherwise known as taiga.

16 January — skare

In Swedish, this is the hard surface layer of snow that forms when melting snow refreezes, beloved by skiers and snowboarders as it can help them to pick up speed. The equivalent English word, 'snow crust', just doesn't cut the mustard.

17 January

nesh

> 'Why en't you cold, Serafina Pekkala?'
>
> 'We feel cold, but we don't mind it, because we will not come to harm. And if we wrapped up against the cold, we wouldn't feel other things, like the bright tingle of the stars, or the music of the Aurora, or best of all the silky feeling of moonlight on our skin. It's worth being cold for that.'

In Philip Pullman's wonderful children's novel *Northern Lights*, Serafina Pekkala is a witch queen from Lake Enara (a parallel to Lake Inari in Sápmi – 'Lapland' – home of the Sami people of the subarctic Fennoscandian Peninsula). To put things scientifically, Serafina's love of the cold – like those who swear by cold water swimming – means that she is not thermosensitive. The novel's plain-speaking heroine, Lyra, might instead say the witch queen isn't 'nesh' – the northern English word used for people who really, really feel the cold.

Do take and don't take Serafina's advice on those winter walks: dress up warm, certainly, but let at least some of your skin drink in the cold winter air.

18 January

murmuration

A murmuration is one of the great sights of autumn and winter skies towards twilight, as hundreds of starlings swoop and dive in acrobatic formation. Sometimes they take the shape of a twisting ribbon, at others a wave, occasionally even a rolling sphere. The collective noun 'a murmuration of starlings' is medieval in origin – from *The Book of St Albans* (1486) – referring to the murmuring sound created by so many beating wings.

Maggie Smith in her poem 'Starlings' memorably describes their aerial acrobatics as 'like a thousand arrows pointing in unison one way, then another.'

19 JANUARY

sastrugi

> Often as we marched the sledges would be brought up all standing by a sastrugus, or snow mound, caused by the wind, and we would be lucky if we were not tripped up ourselves. Small depressions would escape the eye altogether, and when we thought that we were marching along on a level surface, we would suddenly step down two or three feet.

Sastrugi are like the miniature dunes of the Arctic, Antarctic and snow uplands, where the wind sculpts the deep snow into anvil-like ridges. They look spectacular, collectively resembling a sea of frozen waves, but they are a menace to those travelling over them, whether polar explorer or skier. The word is borrowed from Russian, though in this report published in the Hobart, Australia, newspaper *The Mercury* in March 1912, the Norwegian polar explorer Roald Amundsen – the first to reach the South Pole – uses a Latin-like singular.

20 JANUARY

mourie-kaavie

When a plain old blizzard won't do, try out mourie-kaavie, a Scots word for a violent, driving snowstorm. Try to avoid actually being out in one, though.

21 JANUARY

hyperborean

We've already met 'boreal' (15 January), so 'hyperborean' describes anything from the *extreme* north, especially Arctic lands such as Iceland. In Greek mythology the Hyperboreans were a people who lived in a utopian land of plenty and perpetual sunshine beyond the north wind (Boreas). How wrong could the Greeks be!

22 January — ermine

> There are such a lot of things that have no place in summer and autumn and spring. Everything that's a little shy and a little rum. Some kinds of night animals and people that don't fit in with others and that nobody really believes in. They keep out of the way all the year. And then when everything's quiet and white and the nights are long and most people are asleep – then they appear.

Another lovely quotation from Tove Jansson's *Moominland in Midwinter* (see 3 January), highlighting winter as the season for the weird, the wonderful and the downright queer in the animal kingdom. Stoats (*Mustela erminea*) shed their brown coats in autumn, and in the winter are resplendent in white fur – historically making them quarry for hunters who knew them in their white guise as ermine. The mountain hare (*Lepus timidus*) also dons a snow-white winter coat. And we humans get along (just) – with the aid of bobble hats, overlong scarves and zany jumpers.

23 January — reindeer

> These are the days that Reindeer love
> And pranks the Northern star,
> This is the Sun's objective
> And Finland of the year.

– Emily Dickinson

Reindeer – meaning 'horned deer' – are one of the totemic animals of the Arctic and subarctic. In winter, huge herds of reindeer make thousand-mile migrations across the taiga (see 15 January) in search of lichen.

24 JANUARY

nilas

A thin, dark, smooth sheet of ice floating on top of a polar sea that bends and swells with the waves beneath.

25 JANUARY

ice-blink

The whitish glare on low clouds above an accumulation of distant ice.

26 JANUARY

lupine

> It is winter and cold weather. In this region of mountain and forest, there is now nothing for the wolves to eat. Goats and sheep are locked up in the byre, the deer departed for the remaining pasturage on the southern slopes – wolves grow lean and famished. There is so little flesh on them that you could count the starveling ribs through their pelts, if they gave you time before they pounced. Those slavering jaws; the lolling tongue; the rime of saliva on the grizzled chops – of all the teeming perils of the night and the forest, ghosts, hobgoblins, ogres that grill babies upon gridirons, witches that fatten their captives in cages for cannibal tables, the wolf is worst for he cannot listen to reason.

Unlike many animals, wolves (*Canis lupus*, among other species) remain very active in winter, roaming their territory as they hunt down their even more vulnerable prey. In her darkly gothic short story 'The Company of Wolves' – a feminist retelling of the fairy tale 'Little Red Riding Hood' – Angela Carter paints a terrifying depiction of these strange wild animals that are like, and yet unlike, the domestic dog.

Lupine, as everyone knows, is the Latin-derived word meaning 'relating to wolves'; less well known is lupophobia, the irrational fear of these majestic forest hunters.

27 January — snirt

One of the ugliest sights in winter are the banks of dirty snow that pile up at the side of roads. There's a recent American/Canadian portmanteau to describe this: snirt – mushing the two words together just as the snow meets the mud and mess spun up by the passing cars.

28 January — pakkaslumi

The Finns love their snow words: here's another, that means the powdery snow that's perfect for skiers who want the magical sensation of flying through the air.

29 January — katiksugnik

Yesterday the fields were only grey with scattered snow,
And now the longest grass-leaves hardly emerge;
Yet her deep footsteps mark the snow, and go
On towards the pines at the hills' white verge.

I cannot see her, since the mist's white scarf
Obscures the dark wood and the dull orange sky;
But she's waiting, I know, impatient and cold, half
Sobs struggling into her frosty sigh.

Why does she come so promptly, when she must know
That she's only the nearer to the inevitable farewell;
The hill is steep, on the snow my steps are slow –
Why does she come, when she knows what I have to tell?

Winter is usually depicted as a desolate time, not only in nature but for human beings: most of us feel as though January is something to be endured than enjoyed. In his poem 'A Winter's Tale' D H Lawrence associates a snowy landscape with the coming end of a love affair.

Lawrence's image of the woman's footprints marking the snow might make a linguist think of one of the Inuit language's many words for snow: *katiksugnik* means light snow, deep enough for walking.

30 January

snow-bones

Long after the snow has melted, there are sometimes remnants lying by the roadside or in the ridges and furrows of fields – places where the thaw has not quite reached. In northern England these have been known as snow-bones since at least the late 18th century. It's a striking image – suggesting, perhaps, the eerie remains of rime giants' bodies (see 18 November).

31 January

crystalline

> Now the winter's day was set in motion and we rode through its crystal kingdom...We saw trees lopped-off by their burdens of ice, cow-tracks like pot-holes in rock...The church clock had stopped and the weather-cock was frozen, so that both time and the winds were stilled; and nothing, we thought, could be more exciting than this.

Cider with Rosie has the reputation of being an idyllic summer novel, but the young Laurie Lee and his childhood friends also loved winter, as this passage shows.

It's good to end this difficult month on a high note, although for some of us February – the 'mud month' – can be even worse...

February

The snow is gone from cottage tops
The thatch moss glows in brighter green
And eves in quick succession drops
Where grinning ides once hath been.

– John Clare, 'A Thaw'

The Old English name for February – Solmonath – means 'mud month', and there's surely no better name for this soggy, dirty, tiresome time of year. Paths are clogged and slippery, lawns are like bogs, muddy paw prints trail through the house, and the washing machine is eternally whirring: as you'll see through the course of this month, there's no getting away from it: ubiquitous, infuriating mud.

But as the 19th-century English poet John Clare reminds us in his poem 'A Thaw', part of the February section of his *The Shepherd's Calendar*, there are hopeful, if uncertain, signs of change – whether the drip-drop of melting icicles ('ides') conjured in the poem, or the sight of a snowdrop bravely venturing the cold or golden-yellow catkins dancing from a birch. You could almost convince yourself that spring is just around the corner...

1 February

mud

Mud, mud, glorious mud
Nothing quite like it for cooling the blood
So follow me, follow down to the hollow
And there let us wallow in glorious mud.

So, we may as well start with the word 'mud' itself – monosyllabic and onomatopoeic, its very name suggests its primeval nature. It was already a word in Proto-Indian European, where **mū-* probably meant 'moist'. Creation myths are likewise chock-a-block with mud: it is the prime material out of which the earth and even humans are made. Ancient Egyptians, for example, believed that the first gods emerged out of a cosmic muddy soup, reflecting the generative powers of the Nile's muds during the annual floods.

Michael Flanders and Donald Swann's joyous song from 1957 about a hippopotamus and his mud baths may be far indeed from our own experience of February gloop, but it reminds us that mud does have its upsides: after all, it – life – all starts here!

So get out your wellies and enjoy!

2 February

groundhog

In Pennsylvania and surrounding regions 2 February is Groundhog Day. This meteorological superstition says that, if a groundhog (*Marmota monax*, an American species of marmot) emerges from its borrow on this day and sees its shadow – that is, if it's a sunny day – then there will be another four weeks of winter. The superstition was brought to America by German settlers – the Pennsylvania Dutch – and in Germany itself there is a similar tradition involving the native badger, though this is observed on the first of February: *Dachstag*, 'Badger Day'.

Even if there is sunshine on a February day, then, there's even more reason to snuggle under the duvet.

snowdrop

Lone Flower, hemmed in with snows, and white as they
But hardier far, once more I see thee bend
Thy forehead, as if fearful to offend,
Like an unbidden guest. Though day by day
Storms, sallying from the mountain-tops, waylay
The rising sun, and on the plains descend;
Yet art thou welcome, welcome as a friend
Whose zeal outruns his promise! Blue-eyed May
Shall soon behold this border thickly set
With bright jonquils, their odours lavishing
On the soft west-wind and his frolic peers;
Nor will I then thy modest grace forget,
Chaste Snowdrop, venturous harbinger of Spring,
And pensive monitor of fleeting years!

We all look out for the first snowdrops – a sign that there are better things to come than the cold and the mud and the oh-too-brief days, and that we just need to hold out that little bit longer. William Wordsworth's poem 'To a Snowdrop' is a distillation of all that hopefulness and resilience.

The flower's association with snow is widespread: in the French *perce-neige* ('pierce-snow') and the Welsh *eirlys* ('snow lily'). Other local names associate it with the Virgin Mary, as in the Essex name 'Mary's tapers', because the flower appears around the Marian feast of Candlemass on 2 February.

4 February

gubber

By February, autumn's golden treasure of fallen leaves has melted and decayed, adding to the general winter gunkiness. The Sussex dialect has the excellent word 'gubber' to exactly describe this black, rotten mud-matter – indispensable, we need to remind ourselves, for the fecundity of the coming year.

5 February

fill-dyke

February fill the dyke,
Be it black or be it white;
But if it be white,
It's the better to like.

This old country saying suggests that, whether through snowmelt ('white') or heavy rain ('black'), February will be soggy and the ditches filled with water. The melting snow is considered better as it restocks the groundwater more gradually and effectively. The saying is commemorated in the landscape painting *February Fill Dyke,* painted in 1881 by the Worcestershire artist Benjamin Williams Leader, the waterlogged village environs depicted like a kind of corrective to John Constable's idyllic *The Hay Wain*.

nimbostratus

A clamminess hangs over all like a clout,
The fields are a water-colour washed out,
The sky at its rim leaves a chink of light,
Like the lid of a pot that will not close tight.

She is away by the groaning sea,
Strained at the heart, and waiting for me:
Between us our foe from a hid retreat
Is watching, to wither us if we meet . . . .

But it matters little, however we fare –
Whether we meet, or I get not there;
The sky will look the same thereupon,
And the wind and the sea go groaning on.

Poet and novelist Thomas Hardy is the master of pathetic fallacy – the notion that the weather reflects human emotion – and in this poem, 'Suspense', his mastery is in full swing: the winter sky is like a damp old cloth ('clout'), echoing and compounding the narrator's lovelornness and sense of being trapped within a lonely landscape.

In winter, we can all feel as though we are living under an upturned porridge pot, so low and heavy-grey does the cloud hang above our heads. Nothing but rain and snow is in the offing. This type of cloud cover is called nimbostratus – made of the Latin for 'rain cloud' plus 'layer'. My personal coinage would be *gruelostratus*.

There's more Hardy tomorrow – the true poet of mud and mire.

clidga

The bars are thick with drops that show
As they gather themselves from the fog
Life silver buttons ranged in a row,
And as evenly spaced as if measured, although
They fall at the feeblest jog.

They load the leafless hedge hard by,
And the blades of last year's grass,
While the fallow phoughland turned up nigh
In raw rolls, clammy and clogging lie –
Too clogging for feet to pass.

How dry it was on a far-back day
When straws hung the hedge and around,
When amid the sheaves in amorous play
In curtained bonnets and light array
Bloomed a bevy now underground!

We all love winter walks, for the bracing air and the chance to see bright open skies. But what we don't like – well, what I don't like – are the gloopy areas of deep mud that have formed on either side of farm gates – where tractors and livestock and we walkers and our dogs have passed to and fro. There should be a name for them, shouldn't there? Well there is, at least in Cornish – a clidga. Not that being able to name it makes the experience of sinking into a mire while fiddling with a gate latch any better.

Thomas Hardy's poem 'At Middle-Field Gate in February' is the perfect evocation of a Wessex, or West Country, landscape at the mud-end of winter.

8 February

mawkit

After the filthy February walk described in the previous entry we and our dogs may well end up – if we are in Scotland, at least – mawkit, covered head-to-toe in mud. The word likely comes from the Old Norse word for 'maggot' – though hopefully an infestation with maggots is something we won't come home with.

9 February

glaur

> Through glaury holes an' dybes nae mair
> Ye'll ward my pettles frae the lair.

Unsurprisingly, Scots is rich in muddy words. Glaur(y) – with unknown etymology – is here recorded in some peculiarly squelchy lines from 'The Poet's Farewell to His Old Shoes' by Ebenezer Picken. There are no fewer than three mud-related words here: glaur, dybes and lair, all used as the poet bids goodbye to his mud-ruined footwear.

10 February

sugar snow

In the morning the house was warm from the stove, but when Laura looked out of the window she saw that the ground was covered with soft, thick snow. All along the branches of the trees the snow was piled like feathers, and it lay in mounds along the top of the rail fence, and stood up in great, white balls on top of the gate-posts.

Pa came in, shaking the soft snow from his shoulders and stamping it from his boots. 'It's a sugar snow,' he said.

Laura put her tongue quickly to a little bit of the white snow that lay in a fold of his sleeve. It was nothing but wet on her tongue, like any snow. She was glad that nobody had seen her taste it.

In her semi-autobiographical children's book *Little House in the Big Woods*, the young Laura Ingalls Wilder, who died on this day in 1957, learns that sugar snow gets its name because snowfall in early spring delays the maple trees from coming into leaf and causes the sap to run for longer. The overall result: more maple syrup to tap and slather on breakfast pancakes. A cloud, then, with a delicious silver – or more properly golden – lining.

11 February

snow moon

The full moon of February gets its name for obvious reasons – a pretty and evocative one, nonetheless – the silver-white of the moon answering the deep blankets of snow.

12 February

galanthophile

While we laypeople might think there is only one kind of snowdrop, there are in fact as many as 30 wild species – as any galanthophile (snowdrop lover or collector) will tell you. There are some 2,500 cultivated varieties, and shimmering snowdrop displays can be enjoyed in many a park and garden. Of course we all love snowdrops, but there may be a galanthophobe or two out there, poor souls.

13 February

luty

For the Polish, it is February, not April, that it is the cruellest month (see April's introduction). The Polish word for February, *luty*, derives from the Old Polish for 'fierce' or 'cruel'. Try taking a winter walk in the north-east region of Suwałki, where winds blowing across from Siberia keep the daytime temperature well below freezing, and you may well understand why.

14 February

alevin

Forget St Valentine's Day, in Northumberland, 14 February is the traditional date for the Blessing of the Salmon on the chill, broad banks of the Tweed. At this point in their life cycle the salmon –called alevin – are just newly hatched, still attached to a yolk sac, and safe and snug beneath the riverbed's gravel. The word isn't that old, it was borrowed from a French word for young fish only in the mid-19th century.

See 30 April for another stage in the salmon's journey.

ewe-lease

He [Boldwood] descended the stairs and went out towards the gate of a field to the east, leaning over which he paused and looked around.

It was one of the usual slow sunrises of this time of the year, and the sky, pure violet in the zenith, was leaden to the northward, and murky to the east, where, over the snowy down or ewe-lease on Weatherbury Upper Farm, and apparently resting upon the ridge, the only half of the sun yet visible burnt rayless, like a red and flameless fire shining over a white hearthstone. The whole effect resembled a sunset as childhood resembles age.

In other directions, the fields and sky were so much of one colour by the snow, that it was difficult in a hasty glance to tell whereabouts the horizon occurred; and in general there was here, too, that before-mentioned preternatural inversion of light and shade which attends the prospect when the garish brightness commonly in the sky is found on the earth, and the shades of earth are in the sky. Over the west hung the wasting moon, now dull and greenish-yellow, like tarnished brass.

Thomas Hardy's *Far From the Madding Crowd* is a love letter to his native Dorset – masquerading as the fictional county of Wessex. Here farmer William Boldwood is reflecting upon a valentine he himself had received the previous day, but is distracted by the morning's sunrise. Ewe-lease is West Country expression for a pasture in which ewes are kept.

16 February — gutter

The Shetlandic landscape is inspiring even in the depths of winter, but February is not just cold but very, very muddy, so sludgy words abound in the Shetlandic dialect, with its rich input of Old Norse. Gutter is the general word for mud, while a heap of mud is a 'clatch o gutter'. Even the name of the islands' capital, Lerwick, relates to mud: it means 'muddy bay'.

17 February — dumberdash

> The rain came down, straight and silvery, like a punishment of steel rods. It clattered onto the house and onto the rocks and pitted the sea. The thunder made some sounds like grand pianos falling downstairs, then settled to a softer continuous rumble, which was almost drowned by the sound of the rain. The flashes of lightning joined into long illuminations which made the grass a lurid green, the rocks a blazing ochre yellow, as yellow as Gilbert's car.

This passage from Iris Murdoch's 1978 Booker Prize-winning novel *The Sea, the Sea* vividly captures the sights and sounds of a sudden, violent rainstorm. Cheshire dialect has an evocative word for just such a storm – dumberdash – capturing at once the cacophony of thunder and the pelting thrash of rain. A word for any month of the year – at least in the British Isles.

18 February

catkin

The little 'tails' of tightly packed flowers known as catkins appear on a variety of trees, such as poplar, hazel and aspen, from late winter to early spring, bringing sparks of colour to the as-yet leafless trees. The wind carries the pollen from the male catkins to pollinate the female catkins, which then release their seeds. It is their appearance that gives them their name, like little cat's tails or, as in 'The Song of the Hazel-Catkin Fairy' poem by Cicely Mary Barker 'little tails of lambs'.

19 February

chelidonian

> Certain persons give the name Chelidonias to the West wind on the 19th February, owing to the appearance of the swallow [Latin *chelidon*, from the Greek *khelidōn*], but some call it Ornithias, from the arrival of the birds on the 71st day after the shortest day, when it blows for nine days.

The Mediterranean spring arrives rather earlier than the British one, as recorded here in the 1st century AD by Pliny the Elder in his *The Natural History*, but even in the gloom of northern Europe, by 19 February we are likely beginning to feel a bit more cheerful. Chelidonian is used to describe not only a warm spring wind, but also a deep cinnamon colour similar to that found on a swallow's throat.

rivulet

Flow down, cold rivulet, to the sea,
  Thy tribute wave deliver:
No more by thee my steps shall be,
  For ever and for ever.
Flow, softly flow, by lawn and lea,
  A rivulet then a river:
Nowhere by thee my steps shall be
  For ever and for ever.
But here will sigh thine alder tree
  And here thine aspen shiver;
And here by thee will hum the bee,
  For ever and for ever.
A thousand suns will stream on thee,
  A thousand moons will quiver;
But not by thee my steps shall be,
  For ever and for ever.

– Alfred, Lord Tennyson, 'A Farewell'

The diminutive form of river, rivulets are small rivers of water, trickling through the landscape before joining each other as rivers in their rush to the sea.

21 FEBRUARY

kisaragi

Negawaku wa	I wish that
Hana no moto nite	Under the flowers
Haru shinan	I will die in spring
Sono kisaragi no	By the light of the Kisaragi
Mochizuki no koro.	Full moon

February's glimpses of hopefulness can be seen in this poem by the Japanese Buddhist monk-poet Saigyō Hōshi – at least to the extent that he sees his coming death as also offering the promise of regeneration.

Modern Japanese rather prosaically names the month for their order in the year: *ichigatsu* (First Month = January); *nigatsu* (Second Month = February) and so on. The months' traditional, more poetic names have survived, though: February is *kisaragi*, meaning 'changing', presumably in recognition of the month's transition towards spring.

22 FEBRUARY

lutose

As we are in the muddy month, we might as well cover lutose, derived from the Latin for mud, *lutum*. Its use, though, is pretty much confined to entomology, where it describes a mud-like powdery substance found on some insects.

23 FEBRUARY

georgic

While yet the spring is young, while earth unbinds
Her frozen bosom to the western winds;
While mountain snows dissolve against the sun,
And streams, yet new, from precipices run;
Even in this early dawning of the year,
Produce the plough, and yoke the sturdy steer,
And goad him till he groans beneath his toil,
Till the bright share is buried in the soil.

By February the farming year has got under way in earnest, at least in southern Europe, as recorded in the first Georgic by Roman writer Virgil, most famous for his epic *The Aeneid*. The Georgics got their name from the Greek word for farmer, *georgos* – combining the words for 'earth' and 'worker'. Virgil grew up in a well-to-do peasant family, so writes from personal experience of getting his hands dirty. The word 'georgic' today is almost only used in this sense of 'agricultural poetry', though it flourishes, of course, in the name 'George'.

24 FEBRUARY

headrig

On the subject of ploughing, Seamus Heaney's moving tribute to his father, 'Follower', describes his experience stumbling to keep up in the wake of his father as they followed the plough. The headrig – mentioned in the poem – is the unploughed strip of land at the top (or bottom) of a field, where the farmer turned the plough.

25 FEBRUARY

flindrikin

A charming Scots word for a snow flurry, or indeed for any frivolous thing or a trifle. It is one of no fewer than 421 words for snow compiled in the *Historical Thesaurus of Scots*.

26 FEBRUARY

slush

> I'm as pure as the driven slush.

One of the many quips of Hollywood actress Tallulah Bankhead, known as much for her racy lifestyle as for films such as Alfred Hitchcock's *Lifeboat*. 'Slush' is the sound-perfect word for the icy grey mess that forms as snow begins to melt. After the magic of winter white, the world looks all the more monotone. It's at such a sight that February can really get to you.

27 FEBRUARY

celandine

> There is a Flower, the Lesser Celandine,
> That shrinks, like many more, from cold and rain;
> And, the first moment that the sun may shine,
> Bright as the sun himself, 'tis out again!
>
> When hailstones have been falling, swarm on swarm,
> Or blasts the green field and the trees distressed,
> Oft have I seen it muffled up from harm,
> In close self-shelter, like a Thing at rest.

But lately, one rough day, this Flower I passed,
And recognized it, though an altered form,
Now standing forth an offering to the blast,
And buffeted at will by rain and storm.

I stopped, and said, with inly-muttered voice,
'It doth not love the shower, nor seek the cold:
This neither is its courage nor its choice,
But its necessity in being old.

'The sunshine may not cheer it, nor the dew;
It cannot help itself in its decay;
Stiff in its members, withered, changed of hue.'
And, in my spleen, I smiled that it was grey.

To be a Prodigal's Favourite – then worse truth,
A Miser's Pensioner – behold our lot!
O Man, that from thy fair and shining youth
Age might but take the things Youth needed not!

Appearing in late February, the golden-yellow lesser celandine – here immortalized in lines from the well-known poem by William Wordsworth – is a welcome, if precocious, sign of coming spring. The lines are as good an evocation of February's inclement weather and our own mixed responses to this time of year as it of the flower.

Incidentally, celandine is another 'swallow' word (see 19 February), derived (via Norman French) from the Greek *khelidōn* – both flowers and birds have been seen as harbingers of spring since ancient times.

helmikuu

Greeting bring I to the mountains,
Greeting to the vales and uplands,
Greet ye, heights with forests covered,
Greet ye, ever-verdant fir-trees,
Greet ye, groves of whitened aspen,
Greetings bring to those that greet you,
Fields, and streams, and woods of Lapland.
Bring me favour, mountain-woodlands,
Lapland-deserts, show me kindness,
Mighty Tapio, be gracious,
Let me wander through thy forests,
Let me glide along thy rivers,
Let this hunter search thy snow-fields,
Where the wild-moose herds in numbers
Where the bounding reindeer lingers.

In their name for February, which translates as 'pearl month', the ever-poetic Finns draw attention to the beauty of the more abundant sunlight of late winter as it sparkles on frost-covered trees and over the deep snow. February 28 is National Kalevala Day, celebrating the Finnish national epic, *Kalevala* (here translated into English by John Martin Crawford), much of which takes place in cold winter landscapes. In in this passage, the shaman-hero Lemminkäinen prays to Tapio, god of the forests, that his snow-shoes carry him quickly through the frozen wilderness of Lapland.

29 February

slob

March is upon us, and nature and nature's poetry are returning...

...But hold on, one more mud word for Leap Day before February's out. 'Slob' is thick, stodgy mud, the kind that seems to get into every groove and hook of your walking boots.

March

It was one of those March days when the sun shines hot and the wind blows cold: when it is summer in the light, and winter in the shade.

– Charles Dickens, *Great Expectations*

As soon as March arrives we are likely to heave a sigh of relief. Spring, we think, has gained a firm foothold, and there are signs of new life everywhere. Hares get excitable, daffodils parade in every park and the fields are unruly with newborn lambs. Even the soundscape changes, as we begin to wake up to the clamour of birdsong. Our bodies, hearts and minds follow suit, and we feel a surge of optimism – every cliché about spring is true.

We may feel as though winter is now behind us, but it can bite back at any moment, as Charles Dickens records in this line from *Great Expectations*. March, just like 'cruel April' to follow, is an uncertain, even treacherous month. There can be an almost summery warmth at one moment, a storm or cold snap at the next. The country saying says it all: 'In like a lion, out like a lamb: in like a lamb, out like a lion.'

1 March

primavernal

Spring comes in waves, growing from gentle, hesitant budding to full-blown storm of colour. In the UK at least, we might even think of the successive colours of spring – the white, snowdrop spring, the yellow daffodil spring and the mauve spring of April and May when the season is in full swing. The Italian word for spring, *primavera* (literally 'first spring'), seems to recognize this. Riffing on this, the adjective 'primavernal' occasionally pops up in poetic soils.

2 March

Hrēþmōnaþ

The 8th-century monk and writer St Bede tells us that the Old English name for the month of March Hrēþmōnaþ (Rhedmonth) derived from a Saxon goddess named Rheda, but scholars have since noted that variations on the month's name connect it to Old English words for 'stormy' or 'wild'. March is unsettled, and as we will see, not only in terms of its unpredictable weather but also in the jittery and restless behaviours of animals (including human ones) as they wake up after winter sluggishness.

3 March

fool's spring

Once more the changed year's turning wheel returns:
And as a girl sails balanced in the wind,
And now before and now again behind
Stoops as it swoops, with cheek that laughs and burns, –
So Spring comes merry towards me here, but earns
No answering smile from me, whose life is twin'd
With the dead boughs that winter still must bind,
And whom to-day the Spring no more concerns.
Behold, this crocus is a withering flame;
This snowdrop, snow; this apple-blossom's part
To breed the fruit that breeds the serpent's art.
Nay, for these Spring-flowers, turn thy face from them,
Nor stay till on the year's last lily-stem
The white cup shrivels round the golden heart.

Dante Gabriel Rossetti's Sonnet LXXXIII, 'Barren Spring', contrasts the rebirth of nature in spring with his own sadness, and so warns against taking the season at face value, too straightforwardly: March is a deceptive month, liable to see a sudden snap of cold weather even after spring has sprung – a fool's spring (see also 27 March).

4 March

March

It may seem surprising that the name for March in most European languages is named after a god of war, Mars. It may be because the month's weather is still very uncertain, even stormy, as the winter continues its tussle with spring, but for the early Romans Mars was a god of nature, land and fertility as well as of a god of war; only as the Romans themselves turned from being a predominantly farming people to a more soldierly, land-grabbing one was their patron deity identified more closely with the more querulous Greek god of war, Ares, and become more 'martial' in character. March incidentally was also a time when military campaigns were launched.

5 March — eyrie

> 'Farewell,' they [the eagles] cried, 'Wherever you fare till your eyries receive you at the journey's end!' That is the polite thing to say among eagles.

Birds of prey build their nests as early as January, but more typically in February or March – it's best to be prepared for the young ones. The word was once freely applied to the large nest of any bird of prey, especially high up on a mountain crag or a treetop, but over time became associated largely with the homes of eagles, as in this quotation from J R R Tolkien's *The Hobbit*. Gandalf's formulaic reply to the eagles is similarly lovely: 'May the wind under your wings bear you where the sun sails and the moon walks.'

6 March — daffodil

> I wandered lonely as a cloud
> That floats on high o'er vales and hills,
> When all at once I saw a crowd,
> A host, of golden daffodils;
> Beside the lake, beneath the trees,
> Fluttering and dancing in the breeze.
>
> Continuous as the stars that shine
> And twinkle on the milky way,
> They stretched in never-ending line
> Along the margin of a bay:
> Ten thousand saw I at a glance,
> Tossing their heads in sprightly dance.

The waves beside them danced; but they
Out-did the sparkling waves in glee:
A poet could not but be gay,
In such a jocund company:
I gazed – and gazed – but little thought
What wealth the show to me had brought:

For oft, when on my couch I lie
In vacant or in pensive mood,
They flash upon that inward eye
Which is the bliss of solitude;
And then my heart with pleasure fills,
And dances with the daffodils.

Daffodils are everywhere in March, in parks, on road verges, in swathes by rivers and lakes, in tubs by the front door – so they are worth an entry here, even if William Wordsworth's famous poem commemorates a walk taken in April (see 15 April). They are the strongest sign yet that life is returning.

Odd, then, that the word 'daffodil' descends etymologically from asphodel – a very different plant, featuring white, slender-petalled flowers borne on a spike, that in Greek mythology was closely associated with the dead: the Asphodel Fields were the dull and gloomy place where those who had lived unheroic lives went in the afterlife. Still, it will be easy enough to forget that when you next come across 'a crowd, a host, of golden daffodils'.

7 March **hyacinth**

The 7th of March is World Hyacinth Day (everything must have its day in the sun), so what better word today than hyacinth. In ancient Greek the word originally meant a blue-purple gemstone, but was later used for the fragrant spring flower. In her flower poem 'Hyacinth', the Pulitzer Prize-winning poet Louise Glück refers to the mythological young man Hyacinthus, beloved of Apollo, from whose blood the flower grew after he was struck dead by a discus, blown off course by the jealous god of the west wind, Zephyrus (see 9 April).

8 March **yean**

> All young animals are appealing but the lamb has been given an unfair share of charm. The moments come back; of a bitterly cold evening when I had delivered twins on a wind-scoured hillside; the lambs shaking their heads convulsively and within minutes one of them struggling upright and making its way, unsteady, knock-kneed, towards the udder while the other followed resolutely on its knees.
>
> The shepherd, his purpled, weather-roughened face almost hidden by the heavy coat which muffled him to his ears, gave a slow chuckle. 'How the 'ell do they know?'
>
> He had seen it happen thousands of times and he still wondered. So do I.
>
> – James Herriot, *All Creatures Great and Small*

March is peak lambing season, and the fields begin to fill with the heartwarming sight of lambs clustering round their mothers. Ean and yean are two forms of an old verb meaning to give birth to a lamb, and are still used in some rural communities.

There are more sheepish words on 9, 15 and 18 March.

9 March

cade lamb

Mary had a little lamb,
  Its fleece was white as snow.
And everywhere that Mary went,
  The lamb was sure to go.
He followed her to school one day,
  That was against the rule.
It made the children laugh and play
  To see a lamb at school.

Lambs rejected by their mothers and hand-reared in the farm kitchen were once known as cade lambs, but now more often as bummer lambs. The practice is commemorated in the well-known 19th-century American nursery rhyme 'Mary had a little lamb', by Sarah Josepha Hale, who claimed it was based on an experience she had while working as a schoolteacher.

The word 'cade' was once used to describe fallen fruit as well, so the sense may have meant 'cast aside', but was then used to mean 'to care for tenderly' or even 'pamper'. A cade child was a spoiled one!

10 March

corm

Some 'bulbs' aren't true bulbs at all, but swollen underground stems – such as found in springtime flowers including the crocus and cyclamen. Like bulbs, they act as nutrient reserve during the plant's winter downtime but, unlike multilayered, leaved bulbs, they are solid. The little corms that grow from the base – which allow the plant to reproduce – are called cormels.

crocus

They heard the South wind sighing
A murmur of the rain;
And they knew that Earth was longing
To see them all again.

While the snow-drops still were sleeping
Beneath the silent sod;
They felt their new life pulsing
Within the dark, cold clod.

Not a daffodil nor daisy
Had dared to raise its head;
Not a fairhaired dandelion
Peeped timid from its bed;

Though a tremor of the winter
Did shivering through them run;
Yet they lifted up their foreheads
To greet the vernal sun.

And the sunbeams gave them welcome,
As did the morning air—
And scattered o'er their simple robes
Rich tints of beauty rare.

Soon a host of lovely flowers
From vales and woodland burst;
But in all that fair procession
The crocuses were first.

Snowdrop lovers – galanthophiles (see 15 February) – may have something to say about this, but here, in 'The Crocuses', the American poet Frances Ellen Watkins Harper paints a portrait of the crocus as the first flower of spring. Like the snowdrop, they symbolize the resilience of life amid hardship.

12 March

erumpent

Speaking of crocuses, we should recall the word 'erumpent', meaning bursting forth, as in leaves and flowers. The word nicely seems to echo both erupt and rampant – though it is from the Latin verb *ērumpěre* – and conjures up the multicoloured mosaics of crocus that decorate our parks at this time of year.

13 March

worm moon

One of the less pleasant names for a full moon, this month's one gets its name because, as the ground thaws and becomes warmer, the worms wriggle closer to the surface. They make a good feast for the birds, though.

smell fox

A rather unattractive common name for a much-welcomed flower – the wood anemone, or *Anemonoides nemorosa*, whose bright star-like flowers begin to bloom in woodland – especially ancient woodland – in March, and continue through the following months. The flower may be beautiful, but the leaves have a musky smell like the scent of a fox we sometimes catch in our suburban gardens. One of Britain's best and most observant botanical poets, John Clare, focuses on their beauty among the fallen leaves:

The wood anemone through dead oak leaves
And in the thickest woods now blooms anew,
And where the green briar and the bramble weaves
Thick clumps o'green, anemones thicker grew,
And weeping flowers in thousands pearled in dew
People the woods and brakes, hid hollows there,
White, yellow and purple-hued the wide wood through.
What pretty drooping weeping flowers they are:
The clipt-frilled leaves, the slender stalk they bear
On which the drooping flower hangs weeping dew,
How beautiful through April time and May
The woods look, filled with wild anemone;
And every little spinney now looks gay
With flowers mid brushwood and the huge oak tree.

15 March

bellwether

A wether is a castrated male sheep, and a 'bellwether' is a sheep with a bell around its neck, whose jangling sound tells the shepherd where his or her flock is roaming. The word has long since untethered from its original meaning to refer to an indicator for economic, political or legal trend.

bucolic

Come live with me and be my love,
And we will all the pleasures prove,
That Valleys, groves, hills, and fields,
Woods, or steepy mountain yields.

And we will sit upon the Rocks,
Seeing the Shepherds feed their flocks,
By shallow Rivers to whose falls
Melodious birds sing Madrigals.

And I will make thee beds of Roses
And a thousand fragrant posies,
A cap of flowers, and a kirtle
Embroidered all with leaves of Myrtle;

A gown made of the finest wool
Which from our pretty Lambs we pull;
Fair lined slippers for the cold,
With buckles of the purest gold;

A belt of straw and Ivy buds,
With Coral clasps and Amber studs:
And if these pleasures may thee move,
Come live with me, and be my love.

The Shepherds' Swains shall dance and sing
For thy delight each May-morning:
If these delights thy mind may move,
Then live with me, and be my love.

Boukolos was the ancient Greek word for a cowherd and gave its name to the genre of pastoral poetry, the 'bucolic'. Bucolic poetry waxed lyrical about shepherds (rather than the obviously less romantic cowherds) and their lovers, and how pleasant it was to live in the countryside rather than in the corrupt city – especially when you were watching other people do all the hard graft.

The bucolic genre was revived in the Renaissance and beyond, as in Christopher Marlowe's charming poem 'The Passionate Shepherd to His Love'. Today we use the word 'bucolic' broadly to refer to the supposedly idyllic (see 23 March) nature of country life.

17 March

adder

Today is St Patrick's Day, so what better word to address than adder, as the good saint is said to have banished all snakes from the island of Ireland. The Irish for snake is *nathair*, which shares a common origin with the Old English word for the same, *naedre*, which over time lost its 'n' to become adder. *Naedre* was once used for any old snake but is now given to the common European viper (*Vipera berus*), one of the three snake species present in the British Isles (but not Ireland).

In spring we are likely to see much more snake activity, as they wake from hibernation. Druids believed that, in spring, adders sometimes gathered together in a slithery frenzy – a terrifying thought!

18 March

chilver

A female lamb. This very old word is still occasionally heard in southern England. Male lambs, poor wee things, just get to be called the slightly ridiculous 'ram lamb'.

swallow

'Out in the meadows the young grass springs,
  Shivering with sap,' said the larks, 'and we
Shoot into air with our strong young wings,
  Spirally up over level and lea;
Come, O swallows, and fly with us
Now that horizons are luminous!
  Evening and morning, the world of light,
  Spreading and kindling, is infinite!'

Far away, by the sea in the south,
  The hills of olive and slopes of fern
Whiten and glow in the sun's long drouth,
  Under the heavens that beam and burn;
And all the swallows were gathered there,
Flitting about in the fragrant air,
  And caught no call from the larks, but flew
  Flashing under the blinding blue.

Out of the depths of their soft rich throats
  Languidly fluted the thrushes, and said:
'Musical thought in the mild air floats,
  Spring is coming and winter is dead!
Come, O Swallows, and stir the air,
For the buds are all bursting unaware,
  And the drooping eaves and the elm-trees long
  To hear the sound of your low, sweet song.'

– Edmund Gosse, 'The Return of the Swallows'

In the city of San Juan Capistrano in southern California, today sees the annual celebration of the return of the swallows. The arrival of these migratory birds is one of the hallmarks of the return of spring, and has been celebrated by the city's Mission since the 1920s, when the pastor saw a local shopkeeper destroying the swallows' nests in the town and encouraged the birds to flock to his chapel instead.

20 March — lamb-storm

Another word for a 'gowk-storm' (see 10 April) – spare a thought for of all those shivering newborn lambs out in the freezing rain!

21 March — vernal

Restoring Nature, lend thine aid!
And o'er the features of the mind
Renew those colours, that must fade,
When vernal suns forbear to roll,
And endless winter chills the soul.

– Philip Freneau, 'The Vernal Age'

Spring is not instant joy, and here the American poet Philip Freneau pleads with nature to restore his mental wellbeing, left in a state of wintriness. Vernal derives from the Latin for spring and is only widely used in the term 'vernal equinox', usually on or around this day.

22 March — Lent

Today lent, with a capital L, refers to the 40 fasting days before Easter, but in medieval times and beyond the word referred much broadly to spring itself. The word is related to Germanic words for long, and refers to the lengthening days of this time of the year.

idyll

Suddenly an unexpected series of sounds began to be heard in this place up against the sky. They had a clearness which was to be found nowhere in the wind, and a sequence which was to be found nowhere in nature. They were the notes of Farmer Oak's flute.

The tune was not floating unhindered into the open air: it seemed muffled in some way, and was altogether too curtailed in power to spread high or wide. It came from the direction of a small dark object under the plantation hedge – a shepherd's hut – now presenting an outline to which an uninitiated person might have been puzzled to attach either meaning or use.

The image as a whole was that of a small Noah's Ark on a small Ararat, allowing the traditionary outlines and general form of the Ark which are followed by toy-makers – and by these means are established in men's imaginations among their firmest, because earliest impressions – to pass as an approximate pattern. The hut stood on little wheels, which raised its floor about a foot from the ground. Such shepherds' huts are dragged into the fields when the lambing season comes on, to shelter the shepherd in his enforced nightly attendance.

Thomas Hardy's 1847 novel *Far from the Madding Crowd* is the closest the writer came to depicting a rural idyll (he is otherwise known for his gloom-and-doom vision of country life). Its hero is the hunky farmer Gabriel Oak, who is here shown during lambing season biding his time in a hillside shepherd's hut as he oversees his flock.

The word 'idyll' ultimately derives from the ancient Greek for 'little picture', *eidyllion* – used to describe 'picturesque' rural poems.

24 March

chiffchaff

One of the common sights on woodland walks in March is the common chiffchaff (*Phylloscopus collybita*). Like other bird names such as the cuckoo (see 16 April), the chiffchaff's is onomatopoeic – imitating its simple, repetitive chiffchaff song. There are similar-sounding names for the bird in other European languages, such as the Irish *tiuf-teaf*, German *Zilpzalp* and the Welsh *siff-saff*, so it must have been – as it still is – a recognizable spring sound in our ancestors' aural landscape. The Latin genus *Phylloscopus* – leaf-explorer – charmingly suggests the bird's preferred woodland habit.

25 March

pettichap

An old folk name for yesterday's chiffchaff, used by John Clare for his poem 'The Pettichap's Nest' about this springtime returnee:

> Well! In my many walks I've rarely found
> A place less likely for a bird to form
> Its nest close by the rut-gulled wagon-trod road,
> And on the almost barefoot trodden ground,
> With scarce a clump of grass to keep it warm!
> Where not a thistle spreads its spears abroad
> Or prickly bush, to shield it from harms way...
>
> Stop! here's the bird – that woodman at the gap
> Frightened him from the hedge: 'tis olive-green.
> Well! I declare it is the pettichap!
> Not bigger than the wren, and seldom seen.
> I've often found her nest in chance's way,
> When I in pathless woods did idly roam;
> But never did I dream until today
> A spot like this would be her chosen home.

26 March

reverdie

Spring and poetry go together like eggs and bacon, and in medieval times there was a genre of spring poems called 'reverdies', welcoming in this time of regrowth and love. The term comes from the French for 'regreened', and in versifying, it is almost as if the poet-as-shaman is summoning nature out of the bare earth. The tradition of the reverdie has continued into modern times: William Carlos William's sequence *Spring and All*, for example, is a reverdie and also a riposte to T S Elliot's *The Wasteland*, itself a kind of anti-reverdie, emphasizing spring as a kind of mass-delusion (see 8 April).

27 March

blackthorn winter

'Beware the blackthorn winter.'

A blackthorn winter, as referred to in the old country saying, is a cold and frosty snap at the end of March when the blackthorn flowers, although it could also refer to the tree's snowdrift-like appearance in the landscape. Unlike the later-blooming hawthorn (see 20 May), blackthorn blooms before the leaves grow, showing the stark black bark beneath.

28 March

gimmer

The chilver, of 18 March, has grown up to be a gimmer, one year later.

29 March

spindrift

> It was really March; but it was April in its mild air, brisk soft wind, and bright sun, occasionally clouded for a minute; and everything looked so beautiful under the influence of such a sky, the effects of the shadows pursuing each other on the ships at Spithead and the island beyond, with the ever-varying hues of the sea, now at high water, dancing in its glee and dashing against the ramparts with so fine a sound, produced altogether such a combination of charms for Fanny, as made her gradually almost careless of the circumstances under which she felt them.

Jane Austen's heroines are all fond of walking and exercise, and even in the naval port of Plymouth Fanny Price – the diffident heroine of *Mansfield Park*, living in temporary exile with her birth family – is able to get out and about to enjoy the fresh sea air. Down on one of the harbour walls she may have had to dodge the occasional spindrift – the salty, foamy tops of waves caught up and blown by the wind. For a rather more violent version of this weather see spoondrift (8 August).

pelagic

And a good south wind sprung up behind;
The Albatross did follow,
And every day, for food or play,
Came to the mariner's hollo!

In mist or cloud, on mast or shroud,
It perched for vespers nine;
Whiles all the night, through fog-smoke white,
Glimmered the white Moon-shine.

Spring is here and traditionally this was the time to set sail, so let's head farther out to sea and into the open ocean. Here magnificent pelagic birds – petrels, albatrosses and shearwaters – soar over the water, occasionally diving for fish beneath the waves.

Let's hope our journey is better fated than that of the sailors in Samuel Taylor Coleridge's epic poem *The Rime of the Ancient Mariner*, in which an albatross accompanies their ship out of icebound Antarctic waters and into warmer climes.

March hare

Than they begyn to swere [swerve] and to stare,
And be as braynles [brainless] as a Marshe hare,
When they have one [won] their habergon [hauberk] of malt,
They wene to make many a man to halt...

Early spring is mating season for the hare, and boxing – paw-fights – and other excitable behaviours become endemic. Jacks compete with other jacks for the attention of the jills, and not all jills are as keen as the jacks and fend off their suitors. The hare in March, normally well mannered, begins to behave erratically, hence the proverbial expression 'mad as a March hare'. In medieval times the 'madness' of hares was more connected to drunkardness than with mental ill health, if the anonymous Middle English poem 'Here Foloweth Colyn Blowbols Testament' is anything to go by. Here the drinkers have drunk so much beer ('malt') that their bodies are sluggish with it, as if they are wearing armour.

April

Whan that Aprille with his shoures soote,
The droghte of March hath perced to the roote,
And bathed every veyne in swich licóur
Of which vertú engendred is the flour;

– Geoffrey Chaucer, *The Canterbury Tales*

So opens the General Prologue in Geoffrey Chaucer's *The Canterbury Tales*, in which a group of pilgrims set out on their journey from London to the shrine of St Thomas Becket in Canterbury Cathedral. April, for Chaucer, is not just the month of 'showers and flowers', but also high time to set out on the road – whether on pilgrimage (like the Wife of Bath, the Miller et al.), to meet old friends (like Robert Burns, see 1 April), or to fall in love (like Lucy Honeychurch, see 23 April). All nature is stirring, is raring to get going...

As with every month April has its dark, cruel side, too, as T S Eliot takes pleasure in reminding us (see 8 April) – those showers can be surprisingly cold and drenching, and even now winter can still make something of an icy comeback; all human experience can end in disappointment. But 'Courage!', as Lucy is roundly told – get out into nature and enjoy all those growing signs that spring really is finally winning the day.

gowk

> I hope, sometime before we hear the gowk, to have the pleasure of seeing you at Kilmarnock, when I intend we shall have a gill between us.

The Scots word for the common cuckoo (*Cuculus canorus*) is 'gowk', related to the Old English *geác* or *gouc*. The cuckoo, for all its negative associations with parasitism and cuckoldry, is also the bird most associated with spring, its call eagerly listened out for. And, as we see in Robert Burns' 1786 letter to a friend, the wine merchant Robert Muir, spring was a time when people got out and about a little more and saw old acquaintances.

In Scots, a gowk was also a fool, and April Fool's Day was Huntigowk Day, when people were tricked into delivering needless messages, only to be met with the refrain: 'Dinna laugh, dinna smile. Hunt the gowk another mile.'

2 April

April

> The merlin whistles clear an' shrill,
> The whins are oot on haugh an' hill,
> An' blythe by ilka buddin' shaw
> April's up an' buskit braw.

The origins of the word 'April' (Latin *Aprilis*) are much debated, though the most convincing is its connection with the Latin *aperire* (to open) – it's the time of year when flowers and leaves – and human hearts, the sentimental among us might add – open up. Others, more tenuously, have related April's name to the Etruscan goddess Apro, a shortened form of the Greek Aphrodite, the love goddess to whom the month – as a time of fecundity – is sacred.

The roundel 'The Buskin' of April' (The Adornment of April) by the Scottish poet Margaret Winefride Simpson captures all the gaiety and restlessness of this burgeoning month. You may not understand every word but the rhythm alone reels you along.

3 April

brindled cow

In Irish folklore, the days of the brindled cow are the first few days at the April when the weather turns suddenly cold and unseasonal, as if winter is returning. They are named for a fabled brindled cow who was said to have boasted that she had withstood even the harshest weather March had thrown at her and was punished for her hubris when March 'borrowed' days from April to make them freezing, too. There is always more weather to be dished out.

4 April — speet

April is notorious for its sudden drenching showers (Shetlandic: speets), but you'll need your waterproofs even more in Shetland – and your thermals, too – where the 'speets' are chilly to boot. Thunder-speets speak for themselves.

5 April — hurcheon

At this time of the year the hedgehog is waking from its hibernation, even in Scotland where its Scots name is the 'hurcheon'. Something of the Auld Alliance between that country and France can be traced in the name, as it was borrowed from northern French *herichon* – in modern standard French *hérisson*.

Shakespeare, too, used much the same word for the animal – 'urchin'. In *The Tempest*, Prospero threatens Caliban thus: 'Urchins / Shall, for that vast of night that they may work, / All exercise on thee' – tantamount to saying, may nocturnal hedgehogs (or else goblins in the shape of hedgehogs) keep you awake with their spines!

polliwog

Children love to watch the life cycle of a frog, in a school pond or classroom terrarium. The stage they love best, as we all know, is when the tadpoles hatch from the frogspawn – when the newborns are all heads and tails. Tadpole means 'toad-head', but a funnier, more descriptive word still is polliwog, originally *polwygle*, or wiggle-head. An epithet Hilaire Belloc references in his poem 'The Frog' from *The Bad Child's Book of Beasts*.

Be kind and tender to the Frog,
  And do not call him names,
As 'Slimy skin,' or 'Polly-wog,'
  Or likewise 'Ugly James,'
Or 'Gape-a-grin,' or 'Toad-gone-wrong,'
  Or 'Billy Bandy-knees':

The Frog is justly sensitive
  To epithets like these.

No animal will more repay
  A treatment kind and fair;
At least
        so lonely people say
Who keep a frog (and, by the way,
They are extremely rare).

forsythia

This spring as it comes bursts up in bonfires green,
Wild puffing of emerald trees, and flame-filled bushes,
Thorn-blossom lifting in wreaths of smoke between
Where the wood fumes up and the watery, flickering rushes.
I am amazed at this spring, this conflagration
Of green fires lit on the soil of the earth, this blaze
Of growing, and sparks that puff in wild gyration,
Faces of people streaming across my gaze.
And I, what fountain of fire am I among
This leaping combustion of spring? My spirit is tossed
About like a shadow buffeted in the throng
Of flames, a shadow that's gone astray, and is lost.

D H Lawrence's poem 'The Enkindled Spring' celebrates the sheer, unstoppable energy of spring – 'this blaze / Of growing' – that's so fierce that it threatens to overwhelm the narrator. The fieriness might make us think of *Forsythia* – named for the 18th-century Scottish botanist William Forsyth – whose firework-yellow flowers make a brief appearance in our gardens in early spring.

laylock

April is the cruellest month, breeding
Lilacs out of the dead land, mixing
Memory and desire, stirring
Dull roots with spring rain.

Laylock is an old or dialect word for the lilac, which, with its heavy blooms and heady fragrance, is a sure sign that spring is moving towards its peak.

Which came first the colour or the flower? The answer is: both! Lilacs aren't native to the Britain and Ireland, but were introduced into gardens from the Balkans in the 16th century. Their name, too, was borrowed, via various intermediary languages, from Persian *leilaq*, meaning bluish. The colour lilac was in turn first used in English in the 18th century.

T S Eliot's opening for his great modernist poem *The Wasteland*, quoted here, famously riffs on the opening of Chaucer's Prologue to *The Canterbury Tales* (see April's introduction).

9 April

zephyr

Thine azure sister of the Spring shall blow
Her clarion o'er the dreaming earth, and fill
(Driving sweet buds like flocks to feed in air)
With living hues and odours plain and hill.

The Greek god of the west wind was Zephyrus, who in spring caused flowers to bloom (his Roman equivalent, Favonius, was even said to be the mate of the goddess Flora) and had all sorts of associations with spring-like things – swans, hyacinths, love...No wonder he – or the diminutive 'zephyr' – is never far from the vocabulary of classic poets.

References to the Greek gods and the returning fecundity of spring are buried in 'Ode to the West Wind' by poet Percy Bysshe Shelley, who contrasts the fierce autumn wind to its' 'azure sister' who brings scents of new life.

10 April

gowk-storm

The willow boughs are yellow now,
For spring has come again;
The peach-tree buds begin to swell,
Dripping with April rain.

The gray-eyed twilight lingers long,
To meet the starry night;
I walk the darkening lanes alone,
And love the sombre light.

– Elizabeth Stoddard, 'The Willow Boughs Are Yellow Now'

April brings rain as well as wind. A gowk-storm is another word for an April shower, this one Scots, associating the heavy rain with the harbinger of spring, the cuckoo (16 April).

Remember that umbrella, even if the sky is wall-to-wall blue!

11 April — vernalagnia

> It was such a spring day as breathes into a man an ineffable yearning, a painful sweetness, a longing that makes him stand motionless, looking at the leaves or grass, and fling out his arms to embrace he knows not what.
>
> – John Galsworthy, *The Forsyte Saga*

Everything and everyone gets a little perkier in spring: lambs gambol, dogs get restless, birds sing their hearts out, and even we humans get a spring in our step. The sap is rising and the whole world gets frisky. This is spring fever, or *vernalagnia*, from the Latin for 'spring lust'. For a similar sentiment, see 25 April.

12 April — bower

> Oh, how good everything tasted in that bower, with the fresh wind rustling the poplar leaves, sunshine and sweet wood-smells about them, and birds singing overhead! No grown-up dinner party ever had half so much fun.

As trees begin to come into leaf they create shady bowers, perfect dwelling paces for fairies (see 23 June) or children, like Katy Carr and her siblings in Susan Coolidge's beloved children's story *What Katy Did*. The word comes from the Old English *bur* or dwelling, and speaks to an instinct we all have to find a quiet place to rest in nature.

13 April

osprey

I think he'll be to Rome
As is the osprey to the fish, who takes it
By sovereignty of nature.

– William Shakespeare, *Coriolanus*

Here Shakespeare compares the megalomaniacal soldier-hero Coriolanus to the osprey (*Pandion haliaetus*), the fish-eating raptor, which come April is busy laying its eggs. The bird was previously known as a sea hawk or sea eagle, but acquired the name osprey, as a corruption of *avis prede* (bird of prey), in the Middle Ages.

14 April

hyetal

I'll sing you twelve, O
Green grow the rushes, O
What are your twelve, O?
Twelve for the twelve Apostles
Eleven for the eleven who went to heaven,
Ten for the ten commandments,
Nine for the nine bright shiners,
Eight for the April Rainers.
Seven for the seven stars in the sky,
Six for the six proud walkers
Five for the symbols at your door,
Four for the Gospel makers,
Three, three, the rivals,
Two, two, the lily-white boys,
Clothed all in green, O
One is one and all alone
And evermore shall be so.

Hyetal is a rather lovely word to keep in mind for showery April, meaning 'relating to rain'. In Greek mythology the Hyades – 'the rainy ones' – were five weeping nymphs, daughters of Atlas, who were transformed into the star cluster of the same name, which rise with the sun in April. In English the cluster was once known as the 'April Rainers', as recorded in the rather obscure 'Green Grow the Rushes, O', which, like the better-known 'Twelve Days of Christmas', is a cumulative carol.

15 April

daffodils

> I never saw daffodils so beautiful they grew among the mossy stones about and about them, some rested their heads upon these stones as on a pillow for weariness and the rest tossed and reeled and danced and seemed as if they verily laughed with the wind that blew upon them over the Lake, they looked so gay ever glancing ever changing.

Dorothy Wordsworth wrote these lines in her journal for Thursday, 15 April 1802 after a shared walk with her brother the poet William Wordsworth around Ullswater. His famous poem (see 6 March) is recognizably born of the same experience, though his wife, Mary Hutchinson, who was not present on the walk, also contributed some of its lines. Wordsworth's 'Daffodils' poem was thus a family effort and not so 'lonely as a cloud' as it pretends.

16 April

cuckoo

Sumer is icumen in
Lhude sing cuccu
Groweþ sed
and bloweþ med
and springþ þe wde nu
Sing cuccu

Summer has arrived,
Loudly sing, cuckoo!
The seed is growing
And the meadow is blooming,
And the wood is coming into leaf now,
Sing, cuckoo!

Talk of summer may seem a bit previous on 16 April, but it's around this date that you may – if you're very, very lucky now – hear the first (male) cuckoo call. Since medieval times, as recorded in the 'Cuckoo Song' (written in Wessex dialect), its distinctive call has given the bird its name. The Old English name for the bird was *geác* or *gouc* (see 1 April), still preserved and heard in Scots.

17 April

sakura zensen

All through the spring months, the Japanese Meteorological Agency gives updates on the progression of the 'cherry blossom front' (*sakura zensen*) as it moves from Okinawa in the south of the archipelago to Hokkaidō in the north. There are 59 'bellwether' trees, and for a tree to be recorded as beginning to blossom it must have at least five flowers in bloom. The blossom forecast is vital for the holding of *hanami* – flower-viewing parties (see 4 May).

fecundity

The world is charged with the grandeur of God.
  It will flame out, like shining from shook foil;
  It gathers to a greatness, like the ooze of oil
Crushed. Why do men then now not reck his rod?
Generations have trod, have trod, have trod;
  And all is seared with trade; bleared, smeared with toil;
  And wears man's smudge and shares man's smell: the soil
Is bare now, nor can foot feel, being shod.

And for all this, nature is never spent;
  There lives the dearest freshness deep down things;
And though the last lights off the black West went
  Oh, morning, at the brown brink eastward, springs —
Because the Holy Ghost over the bent
  World broods with warm breast and with ah! bright wings.

Gerard Manley Hopkins' poem 'God's Grandeur' honours nature's power of renewal – the 'dearest freshness deep down things' – despite the wear and tear imposed by human beings. (Sadly, we may think differently now.)

The poem was, in fact, written in the depths of winter but is pregnant with the promise of spring, with fecundity – a word that ultimately derives from a Proto-Indo-European root meaning 'to suckle', and thus related to other nurturing words like female and foetus.

19 April — laverock

> Here, where primroses thickest paint the green,
> Hard by this little burnie let us lean.
> Hark how the lavrocks chant aboon our heads!
> How saft the westlin winds sough thro' the reeds.

Is there a more beautifully named bird than the skylark (*Alauda arvensis*), or a more appropriate collective noun than an 'exultation'? For all its modest brown plumage, the lark seems – in its dizzying flight and free-flowing warbling – to encapsulate the joy of spring.

To modern ears, the word also has a playful streak – this term 'to lark about' was originally sailors' slang, meaning to play about high up in a ship's rigging.

The Scots word for lark, lavrock or laverock, is here found in a Scottish pastoral comedy, *The Gentle Shepherd*, by Allan Ramsay while its nickname 'pilgrim of the sky' takes us back to Chaucer.

20 April — Easter

> Eosturmonath has a name which is now translated 'Paschal month', and which was once called after a goddess of theirs named Eostre, in whose honour feasts were celebrated in that month. Now they designate that Paschal season by its name, calling the joys of the new rite by the time-honoured name of the old observance.

In *The Reckoning of Time*, St Bede tells us that the Old English name for April is Eosturmonath – month of the goddess Eostre – which over time was worn down to Easter and gave its name to the Christian festival. Bede is the only historical source for the Saxon goddess, although linguistic scholars have since associated her name with other European deities such as the Greek Eos and the Vedic Ushas, both goddesses of the dawn and, by association, spring.

New beginnings, freshness – we have surely caught April's leitmotif by now?

shivelight

Cloud-puffball, torn tufts, tossed pillows | flaunt forth, then chevy on an air-
built thoroughfare: heaven-roysterers, in gay-gangs | they throng; they glitter in marches.
Down roughcast, down dazzling whitewash, | wherever an elm arches,
Shivelights and shadowtackle in long | lashes lace, lance, and pair.
Delightfully the bright wind boisterous | ropes, wrestles, beats earth bare
Of yestertempest's creases; | in pool and rut peel parches
Squandering ooze to squeezed | dough, crust, dust; stanches, starches
Squadroned masks and manmarks | treadmire toil there
Footfretted in it. Million-fuelèd, | nature's bonfire burns on.

– Gerard Manley Hopkins, 'That Nature Is A Heraclitean Fire And Of The Comfort Of The Resurrection'

On a bright, windy April day, bursts of light chase each other across the forest floor. Poet Gerard Manley Hopkins, writing a few months before his death, captured these long lances of light, coining the words 'shivelight' and 'shadowtackle' to evoke their fleeting qualities.

22 April — tulip

April is mid-season for tulips, flowers first introduced into Central and Western Europe from the Ottoman Empire in the mid-16th century. In the Netherlands, their spectacular beauty led to bulbs being exchanged for spectacular sums in the 17th century – a phenomenon dubbed tulip mania – and then a speculation boom as tulips were sold on forward contracts (much like commodities such as coffee or wheat are today). Tulip prices collapsed in February 1637 and a few traders were ruined.

Tulips may have been the first great market bubble, but are much prettier than dot-com or AI stocks.

23 April — violet

> 'Eccolo!' he exclaimed.
>
> At the same moment the ground gave way, and with a cry she fell out of the wood. Light and beauty enveloped her. She had fallen on to a little open terrace, which was covered with violets from end to end.
>
> 'Courage!' cried her companion, now standing some six feet above. 'Courage and love.'
>
> She did not answer. From her feet the ground sloped sharply into view, and violets ran down in rivulets and streams and cataracts, irrigating the hillside with blue, eddying round the tree stems collecting into pools in the hollows, covering the grass with spots of azure foam. But never again were they in such profusion; this terrace was the well-head, the primal source whence beauty gushed out to water the earth.
>
> Standing at its brink, like a swimmer who prepares, was the good man. But he was not the good man that she had expected, and he was alone.
>
> George had turned at the sound of her arrival. For a moment he contemplated her, as one who had fallen out of heaven. He saw radiant joy in her face, he saw the flowers beat against her dress in blue waves. The bushes above them closed. He stepped quickly forward and kissed her.

Here is one of the great romantic scenes of English literature, and an inspiration for countless Mills & Boon-style writers (including Eleanor Lavish!): a handsome Italian coach driver leads Lucy Honeychurch – heroine of E M Forster's *A Room with a View* – to a field of violets where she finds herself unexpectedly kissed by the Nietzsche-loving railway clerk George Emerson.

The scene takes place in April, when spring is in full flow in Italy. Still, violets of various kinds would already be in bloom in Britain, too, though perhaps not with such profusion as on this Florentine hillside.

24 April — cowslip

> a violent scramble along the banks of the Dronne (I think) which are blue, yellow, and suddenly purple; with bluebells, cowslips and gentians.

Thus wrote the novelist Virginia Woolf to the composer Ethel Smyth in a letter dated 24 April 1931, describing a riverside walk in south-west France with her husband Leonard. In her diary the following day she seems to record a walk along the same route, and how it was interrupted by a sudden thunderstorm. Those April showers again!

Incidentally, the cowslip, meaning 'cow-slop', got its name because it often grew in meadows among the cow dung.

25 April — cordate

Nature is endlessly inventive and nowhere more so than in the shapes of leaves, to which we humans have given fancy Latinate names. Cordate leaves, as found in many popular houseplants, are heart-shaped (Latin *cor* = heart), with the cleft of the heart attached to the stem (obcordate leaves are positioned the other way round).

26 April — spring fever

> Don't you know what that is? It's spring fever. That is what the name of it is. And when you've got it, you want – oh, you don't quite know what it is you DO want, but it just fairly makes your heart ache, you want it so!

So says the ever-exuberant, unputdownable Huckleberry Finn near the beginning of Mark Twain's novel, *Tom Sawyer, Detective*. Spring, he reminds us, is a time of restlessness and hence adventure. We need to be out on the road!

27 April — repullulate

> Old forests, where the gnarly oak stands regnant,
> Bristling with twigs that still repullulate,
> And, swoln with spring, with sappy sweetness pregnant,
> The maple blushes with its leafy weight.

The *recherché* rhyme 'repullulate / weight' in the poem 'Spring' by the American poet Madison Julius Cawein – known as the 'Kentucky Keats' – may impress or depress us, but will likely leave us puzzled, too. Repullulate is from the Latin *repullulare*, meaning 'to bud again'. They sure don't write poems like this anymore, and Cawein wrote some 1,500 of them.

viridescence

> But the privations, or rather the hardships, of Lowood lessened. Spring drew on: she was indeed already come; the frosts of winter had ceased; its snows were melted, its cutting winds ameliorated. My wretched feet, flayed and swollen to lameness by the sharp air of January, began to heal and subside under the gentler breathings of April; the nights and mornings no longer by their Canadian temperature froze the very blood in our veins; we could now endure the play-hour passed in the garden: sometimes on a sunny day it began even to be pleasant and genial, and a greenness grew over those brown beds, which, freshening daily, suggested the thought that Hope traversed them at night, and left each morning brighter traces of her steps. Flowers peeped out amongst the leaves; snow-drops, crocuses, purple auriculas, and golden-eyed pansies. On Thursday afternoons (half-holidays) we now took walks, and found still sweeter flowers opening by the wayside, under the hedges.

Spring heals. Even Lowood, the harsh, dour school attended by the young heroine and narrator of Charlotte Brontë's *Jane Eyre*, softens as the season takes hold. If we are a little bit word-snooty, those peeping leaves and colouring-up flower beds might make us think of the word 'viridescence' – the process of turning green.

29 April — frondescence

The trees have been bare for so long that it always seems miraculous, after a few warmish days, when the leaves unfurl and the landscape turns a pale and tender green. This is when you really, really need to reach for the word 'frondescence' – from the Latin *frondescere*, to turn leafy.

30 April — smolt

In April young salmon – known as smolts – migrate from their native rivers down to the sea. They may be anything from one to three years old. Pilgrims, skylarks, salmon, all...it's time to move on, explore... grow up!

May

What is all this juice and all this joy?

– Gerard Manley Hopkins, 'Spring'

By May, spring is unstoppable. What began as a trickle – a snowdrop here, a cuckoo call there – now flows full pelt. The trees – always tardy – burst into full leaf, rugged headlands blaze with gorse, clouds of hawthorn seem to blow across the hillsides. The world becomes noisy with newborn creatures. It's nature at it most festive...a shout, a cry, of life.

It is the month, too, for poetry and poets, who like birds seem almost compelled to open their mouths (or at least tap away on their computer screens). Every schoolchild is asked to write a poem about spring, and even the word for a collection of poetry – an anthology, from the Greek for 'gathering of flowers' – seems to recognize the deep connection between blooms and words

Like Gerard Manley Hopkins, we may just have the presence of mind to wonder: 'What is all this juice and all this joy?' (see 15 May).

plash

> The traveller from the coast, who, after plodding northward for a score of miles over calcareous downs and corn-lands, suddenly reaches the verge of one of these escarpments, is surprised and delighted to behold, extended like a map beneath him, a country differing absolutely from that which he has passed through. Behind him the hills are open, the sun blazes down upon fields so large as to give an unenclosed character to the landscape, the lanes are white, the hedges low and plashed, the atmosphere colourless. Here, in the valley, the world seems to be constructed upon a smaller and more delicate scale; the fields are mere paddocks, so reduced that from this height their hedgerows appear a network of dark green threads overspreading the paler green of the grass. The atmosphere beneath is languorous, and is so tinged with azure that what artists call the middle distance partakes also of that hue, while the horizon beyond is of the deepest ultramarine.

Landscape is always a character in the novels of Thomas Hardy and, in *Tess of the d'Urbervilles*, he shows us its lush north Dorset setting, the Vale of Blackmoor, even before he introduces us to his protagonist, Tess, as she dances around a maypole on May Day – thereby flagging her deep connection to the land as well as her innocence and purity.

The low plashed hedges here are woven together to form a living fence, the root of the word coming from the Latin *plectere*, to plait or braid.

2 May

bosky

But Grantchester! ah, Grantchester!
There's peace and holy quiet there,
Great clouds along pacific skies,
And men and women with straight eyes,
Lithe children lovelier than a dream,
A bosky wood, a slumbrous stream,
And little kindly winds that creep
Round twilight corners, half asleep.

– Rupert Brooke, 'The Old Vicarage, Grantchester'

Rupert Brooke's most famous non-war poem is this encomium to the Cambridgeshire village of Grantchester, written in May when the poet was in Berlin, Germany. George Orwell castigated it for being 'something worse than sentimental', but it's a hard heart that can resist its nostalgic vision of Edwardian England. The hard-hearted among us might also point out the near tautology of the lovely-sounding 'a bosky wood', since bosky already means 'wooded' or 'bushy'.

3 May

Þrimilcemōnaþ

The St Bede tells us that, in the fifth month, the Anglo-Saxons, like other Germanic peoples, milked their cows three times a day, giving it its name Thrimilcemonath – 'three-milkings month'. This was a time when almost every family kept at least a cow or two, and the abundant grass of the season led to cows producing plenty of rich milk.

4 May

hanami

Hana no kage	In cherry blossom's shade
aka no tanin wa	even those we do not know
nakari keri	are not really strangers

One of the transient joys of spring is the blossoming of fruit trees, which typically lasts only a week or two before the petals fall in pink snow showers. Individual flowers survive only a few precious days. To celebrate the phenomenon, the Japanese hold 'flower-viewing' daytime or night-time picnics beneath flowering cherry trees, a tradition that dates to the Nara period, when it was the plum tree that drew the most admiration.

Here, the monk and haiku master Kobayashi Issa celebrates the sense of community that reigns during a *hanami* (flower viewing). All are welcome, and humanity is shared beneath the blossom trees.

May

This passage from *Fantasticks* – a description of the months in the countryside by the Elizabethan writer Nicholas Breton – describes the idyllic pleasures of May:

> It is now May, and the sweetness of the air refresheth every spirit: the sunny beams give forth fair blossoms, and the dripping clouds water Flora's great garden: the male deer puts out the velvet head, and the pagged doe is near her fawning: the Spa-hawk now is drawn out of the mew, and the fowler makes ready his whittle for the quail: the Lark sets the morning watch and the evening, the nightingale: the Barges, like bowers, keep the streams of the sweet rivers, and the mackerel with the shad are taken prisoners with the sea: the tall young oak is cut down for the maypole: the scythe and the sickle are the movers furniture, and the fair weather makes the labourer merry...It is the month wherein Nature hath her fill of mirth, and the senses are filled with delights. I conclude, it is from the Heavens a grace, and to Earth a gladness.

The month gets its name from the Latin month *Maius*, itself named in honour of the Greek and Roman goddess Maia, the mother of Hermes/Mercury and a deity associated with spring growth and fertility.

6 May

susurrus

> Then, to her dark delight, there was a susurrus. There was no wind, but the leaves on the alder bushes by the river bank began to shake and rustle. So did the reeds. They didn't bend, they just blurred. Everything blurred, as if something had picked up the world and was shaking it.
>
> – Terry Pratchett, *The Wee Free Men*

Tiffany Aching, the young witch in training and protagonist of Terry Pratchett's novel *The Wee Free Men* loves to mull over the word susurrus: 'according to her grandmother's dictionary, it meant "a low soft sound, as of whispering or muttering". Tiffany liked the taste of the word. It made her think of mysterious people in long cloaks whispering important secrets behind a door: *susurrususssurrusss...*'

I think we can all agree with Tiffany that it is wonderfully onomatopoeic word, even if it does herald an invasion of supernatural forces here.

7 May

cow-quaker

A sudden, heavy May rainstorm, which traditionally occurs when the cattle are put out to grass.

8 May

nidify

There's a whole nest of words derived from the Latin *nidus*, meaning nest: nidify (to build a nest); nidicolous (remain in the nest after hatching); nidifugous (leaving the nest); nidulant (nesting). These words may be useful to twitchers and their ilk, but may well be puzzling to the rest of us. We wish we could have found a poem rhyming 'nidicolous' with 'ridiculous'!

9 May

garwhoungle

In spring wetlands, the male bittern has a deep-bass call, like a bassoon playing just two notes. Scots dictionaries record the wonderful word 'garwhoungle' to describe the bittern's plaintive cry, although it sounds almost too good to be true.

dogwood

To dreamy languors and the violet mist
  Of early Spring, the deep sequestered vale
Gives first her paling-blue Miamimist,
  Where blithely pours the cuckoo's annual tale
Of Summer promises and tender green,
  Of a new life and beauty yet unseen.
The forest trees have yet a sighing mouth,
  Where dying winds of March their branches swing,
While upward from the dreamy, sunny South,
  A hand invisible leads on the Spring.

His rounds from bloom to bloom the bee begins
  With flying song, and cowslip wine he sups,
Where to the warm and passing southern winds,
  Azaleas gently swing their yellow cups.
Soon everywhere, with glory through and through,
  The fields will spread with every brilliant hue.
But high o'er all the early floral train,
  Where softness all the arching sky resumes,
The dogwood dancing to the winds' refrain,
  In stainless glory spreads its snowy blooms.

In his poem 'Dogwood Blossoms' the poet George Marion McClellan celebrates the vibrant colours of the season, among them the dazzle-white umbrels (clusters of flowers) of dogwood (*Cornus sanguinea*) – a common shrub or tree in the hedgerows and woodlands of southern Britain. Its name likely comes, not from 'dog', but 'dag' (as in 'dagger') – referring to its straight, strong branches that were traditionally used to make arrows and skewers.

delphinium

> The air is part of the mountain, which does not come to an end with its rock and its soil. It has its own air; and it is to the quality of its air that is due the endless diversity of its colourings. Brown for the most part in themselves, as soon as we see them clothed in air the hills become blue. Every shade of blue, from opalescent milky-white to indigo, is there. They are most opulently blue when rain is in the air. Then the gullies are violet. Gentian and delphinium hues, with fire in them, lurk in the folds.

Nan Shepherd was one of Britain's finest nature writers, and here, in *The Living Mountain*, she describes the quality and colours of the air in her beloved Grampians, where she frequently walked and climbed. The blues she evokes include delphinium blue, the flowers taking their name from the Greek for dolphin, although they are not named for similarity to the dolphin's colour, but rather its shape.

aerial

I caught this morning morning's minion, king-
  dom of daylight's dauphin, dapple-dawn-drawn Falcon, in his riding
  Of the rolling level underneath him steady air, and striding
High there, how he rung upon the rein of a wimpling wing
In his ecstasy! then off, off forth on swing,
  As a skate's heel sweeps smooth on a bow-bend: the hurl and gliding
  Rebuffed the big wind. My heart in hiding
Stirred for a bird, – the achieve of, the mastery of the thing!

The word aerial, from the Greek for air, can be applied to anything pertaining to the air, as in the aerial manoeuvres of the kestrel observed by Gerard Manley Hopkins in his poem 'The Windhover'. But figuratively the word also evokes graceful beauty, something we can all become lost in, watching the flight of birds.

13 May — petrichor

Leaving her instructions with Gabriel and Maryann, that they were to see everything carefully locked up for the night, she went out of the house just at the close of a timely thunder-shower, which had refined the air, and daintily bathed the coat of the land, though all beneath was dry as ever. Freshness was exhaled in an essence from the varied contours of bank and hollow, as if the earth breathed maiden breath; and the pleased birds were hymning to the scene.

– Thomas Hardy, *Far From the Madding Crowd*

A relatively recent coinage, first used by Australian scientists in the 1960s, the word 'petrichor' refers to the sweet, fresh smell that rises from the ground after rainfall – created by the release of plant oils and the organic compound geosmin found in soil-dwelling bacteria. The word is derived from the Greek words *petros*, stone, and *ichor*, the fluid that ran through the Olympian gods' veins.

14 May — rill

Rills occur during and after heavy rain, when waters runs off the land or down tracks in narrow groves, created by erosion.

thrush

Nothing is so beautiful as Spring –
  When weeds, in wheels, shoot long and lovely and lush;
Thrush's eggs look little low heavens, and thrush
  Through the echoing timber does so rinse and wring
The ear, it strikes like lightnings to hear him sing;
  The glassy peartree leaves and blooms, they brush
The descending blue; that blue is all in a rush
  With richness; the racing lambs too have fair their fling.

What is all this juice and all this joy?
  A strain of the earth's sweet being in the beginning
In Eden garden. – Have, get, before it cloy,
  Before it cloud, Christ, lord, and sour with sinning,
Innocent mind and Mayday in girl and boy,
  Most, O maid's child, thy choice and worthy the winning.

For all of us, May is a time when we think we can begin life afresh, with a clean slate – much more so, indeed, than at the traditional time of new beginnings and resolutions at New Year. For the Jesuit poet Gerard Manley Hopkins, in his poem 'Spring', the month has an Edenic quality – a time when we can – we must! – all partake in nature's innocence. His totemic bird here is the song thrush (*Turdus philomelos*) whose song dapples and flits through the Maytime woods.

Be warned, however: summer, like our innocence, will soon grow old and stale – 'Have, get, before it cloy.'

16 May — form

> In the black furrow of a field
> I saw an old witch-hare this night;
> And she cocked a lissome ear,
> And she eyed the moon so bright

Hares, unlike rabbits, do not live in warrens but get their rest instead in shallow depressions in the ground, called forms. A form is usually enough to conceal their whereabouts from predators, but, if not, then the hare's speedy-footedness should hopefully get it out of danger's way. Walter de la Mare's poem 'Hare' evokes the folk superstition that witches could turn themselves into hares.

17 May — holt

To raise their young, or to provide shelter, otters build holts in river-banks or among the roots of big old trees, using branches, ferns, reeds and leaves to line a burrow or natural cavity. Otters give birth to their pups all year round, but May to August is peak season.

The word 'holt' meant a copse or thicket in Old English and is found in many old place names, but perhaps also influential is the meaning 'fortified place', as in stronghold.

18 May

drey

More animal homes. Squirrels usually have two litters, the first perhaps in February, the second, say, in May. The blind and hairless kits are nursed by their mother in nests, or dreys, perilously balanced among the branches of trees. Poet Laureate Simon Armitage dedicated his collection of poetry *Dwell* to evocative descriptions of the fragile dwellings of the creatures around us, and managed to capture the precariousness of animal life in his image of the squirrel's 'twig-and-leaf crow's nest squat'.

19 May

dumbledores

Before it was the name of a famous wizard, dumbledore was a common dialect name for the bumblebee. The queen bumblebee comes out of hibernation in late February or March, but by late spring the striped worker bees are busy collecting nectar and pollen from the abundant flowers.

In his Hobbit poem 'Errantry', included in *The Adventures of Tom Bombadil*, J R R Tolkien gives the name 'Dumbledor' to some ferocious oversize insects that haunt the marshlands of Middle-earth.

hawthorn

> My mother, after searching everywhere for me, found me standing in tears on the steep little path near Tansonville, bidding farewell to my hawthorns, clasping their sharp branches in my arms... 'Oh, my poor little hawthorns,' I was assuring them through my sobs, 'it isn't you who want me to be unhappy, to force me to leave you. You, you've never done me any harm. So I shall always love you.' And, drying my eyes, I promised them that, when I grew up, I would never copy the foolish example of other men, but that even in Paris, on fine spring days, instead of paying calls and listening to silly talk, I would set off for the country to see the first hawthorn-trees in bloom.

We've crossed the English Channel here, though only as far as Normandy. This tender scene takes place early on in Marcel Proust's *À la recherche du temps perdu* (In Search of Lost Time) when the young Marcel is uneager to leave his childhood holiday home in the fictional village of Combray. The palest-pink, cloudlike hawthorn – sometimes known as may after the month in which it blooms – is here associated with both innocence and an appreciation of beauty.

The English word means 'hedge-thorn', referring to hawthorn's common usage from Anglo-Saxon times as a field marker (it is still common in hedges today). Incidentally, in French it is *aubépine*, meaning 'whitethorn'.

21 May — furze

> The hills are heathy, save that swelling slope,
> Which hath a gay and gorgeous covering on,
> All golden with the never-bloomless furze,
> Which now blooms most profusely

On late-spring hilly rambles, blazes of yellow gorse alternate with pale-pink clouds of hawthorn and the air about fills with the strong honey-cum-coconut fragrance of gorse flowers. In his poetic description of the Quantock Hills near Nether Stowey (often the title of this 1798 poem) Samuel Taylor Coleridge uses the name 'furze' for this well-known prickly bush; the word also gives us the wonderful adjective 'furzy', where 'gorsy' just wouldn't do.

For more gorsy words, see 24 and 29 May.

22 May — daisy

> Wee, modest, crimson-tippèd flow'r,
> Thou's met me in an evil hour;
> For I maun crush amang the stoure
>   Thy slender stem:
> To spare thee now is past my pow'r,
>   Thou bonie gem.
>
> Alas! it's no thy neibor sweet,
> The bonie lark, companion meet,
> Bending thee 'mang the dewy weet
>   Wi' spreck'd breast,
> When upward-springing, blythe, to greet
>   The purpling east.

Cauld blew the bitter-biting north
Upon thy early, humble birth;
Yet cheerfully thou glinted forth
  Amid the storm,
Scarce rear'd above the parent-earth
  Thy tender form.

The flaunting flowers our gardens yield
High shelt'ring woods an' wa's maun shield:
But thou, beneath the random bield
  O' clod or stane,
Adorns the histie stibble-field
  Unseen, alane.

There, in thy scanty mantle clad,
Thy snawie-bosom sun-ward spread,
Thou lifts thy unassuming head
  In humble guise;
But now the share uptears thy bed,
  And low thou lies!

Robert Burns' poem 'To a Mountain Daisy' is an ode to that most May-ish of flowers, the daisy, which, come that month, begins to flower on lawns and verges everywhere. For Burns, it is also the simplest, the most innocent and most vulnerable of flowers, and thus a symbol, too, of human mortality.

Its name derives from the Old English *dæges ēage*, or 'day's eye', since it opens in the morning and closes at night, mimicking – both in behaviour and looks – the sun. Humble things can also be great things.

23 May — gowan'd

At this time of the year, lawns and fields became 'gowan'd' – meaning 'spangled with daises' in Scots. Gowan is the generic Scots word for a daisy, with 'ewe-gowan' being the common daisy (*Bellis perennis*) because daisies grow among the grazing sheep.

24 May — gorse

Gorse flourishes on the wild, heathy coastlines of the old Celtic lands – Ireland, Wales, Cornwall and Brittany. In such places, the abundant shrub was used as a fuel for bread ovens and stored for winter fodder.

25 May — rhizome

English novelist and poet Helen Dunmore's moving poem 'Hold out your arms' – written on 25 May 2017, shortly before her early death – brims with memories of childhood and spring. In it she likens death to an iris standing by a wall and herself to a child, waiting to be lifted, as by death or by a mother, 'as a rhizome must lift a flower'. Rhizomes are the underground stems of plants such as iris and lily of the valley that spread horizontally beneath the ground, sending out new shoots into the light in spring – and thus a poignant image of the cycle of life, even when death seems to hold sway.

summer

Shall I compare thee to a summer's day?
Thou art more lovely and more temperate:
Rough winds do shake the darling buds of May,
And summer's lease hath all too short a date;

Sometime too hot the eye of heaven shines,
And often is his gold complexion dimm'd;
And every fair from fair sometime declines,
By chance or nature's changing course untrimm'd;

But thy eternal summer shall not fade,
Nor lose possession of that fair thou ow'st;
Nor shall death brag thou wander'st in his shade,
When in eternal lines to time thou grow'st:

So long as men can breathe or eyes can see,
So long lives this, and this gives life to thee.

This is the most famous of Shakespeare's Sonnets (no. 18), on the tip of everyone's tongue and the source of several book and TV titles. While by modern measures – meteorological and astronomical – we are not yet in summer, in old calendars summer often began on 1 May, a tradition Shakespeare follows here. Emotionally, too, by late May we are certainly feeling summery.

Against expectation, the word 'summer' has nothing to do with the sun, though the word certainly helps contribute to the season's pleasant associations. Instead, it derives from a Proto-Indo-European root, *sm-, meaning 'one' – possibly referring to a year and linked to the old tradition of measuring one's age in summers.

27 May

quickthorn

Another name given to the hawthorn (see 20 May), due its quick, sturdy growing – another reason why it has long been used for field boundaries.

28 May

quickbeam

> I am Bregalad, that is Quickbeam in your language. But it is only a nickname, of course. They have called me that ever since I said yes to an elder Ent before he had finished his question. Also I drink quickly, and go out while some are still wetting their beards.

In Old English *-beám* meant tree, and is still used for a sturdy length of timber (the modern German for tree is the cognate *Baum*), and the quickbeam (*cwic-beám*) was the old name for the rowan tree. The tree was thought to be very hardy and long-lived, so the quick here meant 'living' rather than fast, as survives in the phrase the quick and the dead.

J R R Tolkien calls one of his Ents – his tree-people or spirits – Quickbeam. The Ents are notorious for their slowness when it comes to deciding or taking action and so here plays on the double meaning of this young and hasty Ent's name.

29 May

whin

> Sweet as the breath of the whin
> Is the thought of my love

In his plain-speaking love poem 'Sweet as the Breath of the Whin' the World War I poet Wilfred Wilson Gibson uses the northern English and Scots name for gorse (*Ulex europaeus*) – whin. The word derives from Old Norse *hvein*, swamp, where the plant might grow.

30 May

mogshade

Like petrichor (13 May), this word crops up regularly in lists of forgotten words ripe for 'rediscovery', now almost to the extent it seems old hat. It's lovely for all that, and means the dappled pattern of light and shadow thrown by trees in leaf.

31 May

peregrine

Ah, the end of spring – and the day commemorating the Visitation – the Virgin Mary's visit to her cousin Elizabeth, each of them unexpectedly pregnant with child, Jesus and John the Baptist respectively. A good day, then, to bring up the peregrine falcon (*Falco peregrinus*), whose species name means 'traveller' or wanderer'. May is the peak time to watch peregrine chicks being fed by their parents in steeple, tower and cliff-side nests. Soon they will be taking their first fledging flight, out into the blue skies of summer...

June

Too short the lovely summer night,
Too soon 'tis passed away;
I watched to see behind which cloud
The moon would chance to stay,
And here's the dawn of day!

– Kiyohara no Fukayabu

Summer is well and truly here: the year, like the sun itself, reaches its height in June. The growth that gathered then accelerated through spring now reaches its fullness, with, as yet, no sign of the exhaustion that can set in July and August. Every bird, every plant, every insect, seems to brim, sing, hum with energy. Rivers and streams run high. Nature's colour is at its brightest, its volume turned to its highest.

And yet there can be moments of hush and stillness in June – when the midday sun is hot, nature comes to a standstill; or at night, when reality and dream become inseparable, as in Shakespeare's play *A Midsummer Night's Dream*.

June is the month of magic and mayhem.

riggwelter

> It was the first day of June, and the sheep-shearing season culminated, the landscape, even to the leanest pasture, being all health and colour. Every green was young, every pore was open, and every stalk was swollen with racing currents of juice. God was palpably present in the country, and the devil had gone with the world to town. Flossy catkins of the later kinds, fern-sprouts like bishops' croziers, the square-headed moschatel, the odd cuckoo-pint, – like an apoplectic saint in a niche of malachite, – snow-white ladies'-smocks, the toothwort, approximating to human flesh, the enchanter's night-shade, and the black-petaled doleful-bells, were among the quainter objects of the vegetable world in and about Weatherbury at this teeming time.

So begins, in Thomas Hardy's *Far from the Madding Crowd*, the famous sheep-shearing scene where the heroine, Bathsheba Everdene, works alongside, and grows a little closer to, the steadfast shepherd Gabriel Oak.

Sheep-shearing is an important time in the farming calendar – relieving sheep of their heavy winter fleeces and producing a valuable commodity for the farmer in the form of wool. Allowing the fleece to grow too unruly can be dangerous for a sheep's health, owing to the risk of overheating and maggot infestation (flystrike). The weight of a sheep's fleece can even make the animal topple over on its back, leaving it panicked and stranded – in Yorkshire dialect, such a sheep is a riggwelter.

2 JUNE estival

> Summer, June summer, with the green back on earth and the whole world unlocked and seething – like winter, it came suddenly and one knew it in bed, almost before waking up; with cuckoos and pigeons hollowing the woods since daylight and the chipping of tits in the pear-blossom.

This passage from Laurie Lee's *Cider with Rosie* captures the intoxicating essence of summer – the full light, the luxuriance of life, the intensity of birdsong. This is the summer of our childhoods, if we are lucky enough to have brought up in the countryside.

Estival is complementary to autumnal, hibernal and vernal, but only autumnal is of any much use in ordinary speech. Still, an 'estival festival' might be fun.

3 JUNE Ærraliða

Roll on the summer. The mild weather of June and July earned them a joint name in Old English – *Liða*, meaning gentle – as if all those long, easy summer days flowed into one. Those more particular about the passing of time separated them into two: Ærraliða and Æfteraliða, Before- and After-liða.

4 June

piebald

Brimming with leaves and sunshine, light and shadow, June seems to be an appropriate month to quote Gerard Manley Hopkins' joyous poem 'Pied Beauty':

Glory be to God for dappled things –
For skies of couple-colour as a brinded cow;
For rose-moles all in stipple upon trout that swim;
Fresh-firecoal chestnut-falls; finches' wings;
Landscape plotted and pieced – fold, fallow, and plough;
And áll trádes, their gear and tackle and trim.

All things counter, original, spare, strange;
Whatever is fickle, freckled (who knows how?)
With swift, slow; sweet, sour; adazzle, dim;
He fathers-forth whose beauty is past change:
Praise him.

The 'pied' in Hopkins' title, applied to animals such as horses and birds, means 'with black-and-white patches', like a magpie (see 26 June).

5 June

sobremesa

We can linger after a meal at any time of year, of course, but when better than on long summer evenings when the sizzing heat has given way to pleasant warmth, the kinder light flatters, and all seems right with the world. The Spanish have made such postprandial lingering an institution, an artform – the *sobremesa*, meaning 'on the table'. Another glass of wine, another morsel of cheese, amigo?

6 June

birken

Beorc byþ bleda leas, bereþ efne swa ðeah
tanas butan tudder, biþ on telgum wlitig,
heah on helme hrysted fægere,
geloden leafum, lyfte getenge

[The poplar/birch] bears no fruit; yet without seed it brings forth suckers,
for it is generated from its leaves.
Splendid are its branches and gloriously adorned
its lofty crown which reaches to the skies

Thus the 8th- or 9th-century verse known as 'Old English Rune Poem', here translated by Bruce Dickins, evokes a tree, translated variously as either birch or poplar. Certainly the tree described seems closer to a poplar, which reproduces via suckers, but the rune *beorc* is the source of the modern English word birch. Like many tree names, the related adjective is formed by adding *-en* – as in the rather lovely birken, scandalously underused except in the name of the Wirral port of Birkenhead – 'headland of the birches'.

vespertine

It is the French poet Paul Verlaine who provides the best evocation of this word, in his poem 'L'heure exquise' (The Exquisite Hour) – here given in French and in my translation:

La lune blanche	The white moon
Luit dans les bois;	shines in the woods;
De chaque branche	from every branch
Part une voix	comes a voice
Sous la ramée...	beneath the bough...
Ô bien aimée.	O well-beloved.
L'étang reflète,	The pond reflects,
Profond miroir,	deep mirror,
La silhouette	the silhouette
Du saule noir	of the black willow
Où le vent pleure...	where the wind weeps...
Rêvons, c'est l'heure.	Let's dream, it's the hour.
Un vaste et tendre	A vast and tender
Apaisement	calm seems
Semble descendre	to descend
Du firmament	from the firmament
Que l'astre irise...	made iridescent by the star...
C'est l'heure exquise.	It is the exquisite hour.

Vespertine comes from the Latin word for evening, *vesper*, and is most often use to describe animals and flowers that are specifically active as this time (so not necessarily nocturnal). See also nycterine on 13 June.

8 June

skewbald

A skewbald horse is one with a non-black base coat splotched with white (see 4 June – piebald). The skew part of the word is clear; the -bald bit means a 'shining white patch', and thus also the sense of hairless!

9 June

cloudlet

Yes. I remember Adlestrop –
The name, because one afternoon
Of heat the express-train drew up there
Unwontedly. It was late June.

The steam hissed. Someone cleared his throat.
No one left and no one came
On the bare platform. What I saw
Was Adlestrop – only the name

And willows, willow-herb, and grass,
And meadowsweet, and haycocks dry,
No whit less still and lonely fair
Than the high cloudlets in the sky.

And for that minute a blackbird sang
Close by, and round him, mistier,
Farther and farther, all the birds
Of Oxfordshire and Gloucestershire.

In his poem 'Adlestrop', the poet Edward Thomas recalls a blissful moment when the Paddington–Malvern train he was travelling on briefly stopped at this Gloucestershire village, in June 1914. The poem, with its glorious evocation of an 'unspoiled' England countryside, was written the following year, when the war gave the moment additional poignancy. The station closed in 1966.

10 June **strawberry moon**

The full moon in June is the strawberry moon, when the first crops of British strawberries are picked. It's the month, too, of Wimbledon, the tennis championships where spectators eat some 28,000kg (61,730lb) of them. See also 20 June for more strawberries.

11 June **woak**

> Ithin the woodlands, flow'ry gleaded,
> By the woak tree's mossy moot,
> The sheenen grass-bleades, timber-sheaded,
> Now do quiver under voot

One of the finest pleasures of summer is sitting under the canopy of a tree, enjoying the dappled shade, while seeing the world about bathed in sunshine and the sky through the play of leaves above. These lines from the Dorset-dialect poem 'My Orcha'd in Linden Lea' by William Barnes include this local word for oak.

dandelion

O dandelion, rich and haughty,
King of village flowers!
Each day is coronation time,
You have no humble hours.
I like to see you bring a troop
To beat the blue-grass spears,
To scorn the lawn-mower that would be
Like fate's triumphant shears.
Your yellow heads are cut away,
It seems your reign is o'er.
By noon you raise a sea of stars
More golden than before.

– Vachel Lindsay, 'The Dandelion'

Lawn lovers may hate the very sight of the common dandelion (*Taraxacum officinale*), which by June is popping everywhere. But the nature lover will see them, not as weeds, but as little soil conditioners, adding calcium to the earth; cooks, too, will appreciate their bitter leaves in salads; and children will love them when, as 'dandelion clocks' – seedheads – they can be blown to tell the time (or so folklore says). Poets, finally, will treasure them as compact distillations of the joys of summer, as in Vachel Lindsay's poem quoted here.

Everyone knows the etymology of the English flower name from the French *dent de lion* ('lion's tooth'), though the French more crudely call it the *pissenlit* (piss-a-bed), for the diuretic properties of its leaves and roots.

13 JUNE

nycterine

At night-time, nature is heightened – go for a walk at twilight and your senses will be wakened by the scents and sounds around you. Some flowering plants, like the moonflower (*Ipomoea alba*) or the evening primrose (*Oenothera biennis*), open and become fragrant in the evening to attract moths and other nocturnal pollinators. Some animals, too – like bats or owls or mice – start to fly about or rummage around in the undergrowth. All these we might describe as 'nycterine' – from the ancient Greek *nyx*, night – though the word has fallen into disuse. You might like to describe yourself thus, too, if you're a night-owl!

14 JUNE

crepuscular

E E Cummings' haunting, dreamy poem 'Crepuscule' imagines the resurrection of his body in the natural world. Crepuscular comes from the Latin *crepusculum* and is most often used to describe animals active betwixt night and day. See 7 and 13 June.

15 June

nouryou

> The twilight dim, the gentle breeze
> By Nara's little stream,
> The splash of worshippers who wash
> Before the shrine, all seem
> A perfect summer's dream.

A Japanese word describing the practice of taking the time, after daytime heat, to enjoy the cooling evening breeze, especially by a river. The Japanese waka poet Fujiwara no Ietaka captures the sense in a few distilled words.

16 June

pavonine

> My heart, like a peacock on a rainy day,
> spreads its plumes tinged with rapturous colours of thoughts,
> and in its ecstasy seeks some vision in the sky, –
> with a longing for one whom it does not know.
> My heart dances.

So begins Bengali poet Rabindranath Tagore's poem celebrating the arrival of the summer monsoon rains in his home country. In Britain, we might not feel so joyous when it rains in summer (after all, it happens so often), but, as in South Asia, summer showers keep nature fresh and nurtures crops.

Peafowl, in any case, are birds closely associated with summer. On English country estates the peacock's strange, sad cries fill the air and his dazzling fantail brings a dash of Asian opulence to the landscape as he vainly seeks for a mate. The rarely used adjective is pavonine, from the Latin *pavo*, whence also the 'pea' of peafowl. Pavonine would be a great way, perhaps, to describe men out on the town on a summer's night, strutting their stuff in their finery.

17 June

martlet

This guest of summer,
The temple-haunting martlet, does approve
By his loved mansionry that the heaven's breath
Smells wooingly here.

Banquo, in Shakespeare's *Macbeth*, is here welcoming King Duncan to the Macbeths' castle home. Their home must be a good place to stay, he says, because martlets – in all likelihood house martins – like to nest here. How wrong could good Banquo be!

18 June

beechen

Tis not through envy of thy happy lot,
  But being too happy in thine happiness,–
    That thou, light-winged Dryad of the trees
      In some melodious plot
    Of beechen green, and shadows numberless,
      Singest of summer in full-throated ease.

We've met birken – another -en adjective words for trees – and here is 'beechen' in John Keats' melodious 'Ode to a Nightingale'.

rose

With its full blooms, intense colour and heady perfume, the rose (the genus *Rosa*) has been the emblematic flower of summer since ancient times. They have also been the symbol of love, whether fleeting passion or enduring commitment, as in Robert Burns' well-known poem:

O my Luve is like a red, red rose
 That's newly sprung in June;
O my Luve is like the melody
 That's sweetly played in tune.

So fair art thou, my bonnie lass,
 So deep in luve am I;
And I will luve thee still, my dear,
 Till a' the seas gang dry.

Till a' the seas gang dry, my dear,
 And the rocks melt wi' the sun;
I will love thee still, my dear,
 While the sands o' life shall run

And fare thee weel, my only luve!
 And fare thee weel awhile!
And I will come again, my luve,
 Though it were ten thousand mile.

The word itself, too, is very ancient, traceable back to ancient Persian. Roses were cultivated in the royal gardens of Sumer some 5,000 years ago, as well as in China and Egypt.

strawberry

'... I shall wear a large bonnet, and bring one of my little baskets hanging on my arm. Here, – probably this basket with pink ribbon. Nothing can be more simple, you see. And Jane will have such another. There is to be no form or parade – a sort of gipsy party. We are to walk about your gardens, and gather the strawberries ourselves, and sit under trees;– and whatever else you may like to provide, it is to be all out of doors – a table spread in the shade, you know. Every thing as natural and simple as possible. Is not that your idea?'

'Not quite. My idea of the simple and the natural will be to have the table spread in the dining-room. The nature and the simplicity of gentlemen and ladies, with their servants and furniture, I think is best observed by meals within doors. When you are tired of eating strawberries in the garden, there shall be cold meat in the house.'

In this exchange in Jane Austen's *Emma* (1815), would-be fashionista Mrs Elton – the vicar's new wife – and the sensible Mr Knightley – the novel's hero – debate how best to hold a strawberry-picking afternoon on the latter's country estate, Donwell Abbey. Mrs Elton wants to do it Marie-Antoinette style, with the gentry playing at being 'simple' country folk; Knightley will have none of it and gently mocks the lady's pretensions.

The fruit's name is much less likely to come from 'straw' than from 'strewn', describing how the berry grows across the ground, via horizontal stems called stolons. As it turns out, Mrs Elton soon tires of stooping down to pick the strawberries on Mr Knightley's strawberry patch. It's hard work, country life.

21 June

solstice

Above me spreads the hot, blue mid-day sky,
Far down the hillside lies the sleeping lake
Lazily reflecting back the sun,
And scarcely ruffled by the little breeze
Which wanders idly through the nodding ferns.
The blue crest of the distant mountain, tops
The green crest of the hill on which I sit;
And it is summer, glorious, deep-toned summer,
The very crown of nature's changing year
When all her surging life is at its full.

What better way to celebrate the solstice than this passage from Amy Lowell's poem 'Summer'? The word 'solstice' means 'sun-still' or 'sun-stop', and on a blazing summer's day it can indeed seem as if nature has stopped in its tracks: everything pays homage to the commanding sun.

The date of the actual summer solstice varies between the 20th and 22nd, even if midsummer celebrations are held on Midsummer's Eve (23rd) and Midsummer's Day (24th). Does the 21st mark the height of summer, or is it just the beginning? It's all very confusing!

22 June

sólarfrí

In summer we really need to seize the day, and make the most of the fine weather. Nowhere more so than in Iceland, where the weather can be unrelenting and winters are very long. For this reason, when the weather is exceptionally fine, employers may declare a *sólarfrí* – a 'sun holiday' – and employees are set free to get out and enjoy.

23 June — eglantine

I know a bank where the wild thyme blows,
Where oxlips and the nodding violet grows,
Quite over-canopied with luscious woodbine,
With sweet musk-roses and with eglantine

In Shakespeare's *A Midsummer Night's Dream*, the fairy king Oberon describes the bower where his wife, Titania, spends her nights, so that his servant, Robin Goodfellow or 'Puck', can pour a love potion into her eyes. The eglantine is the sweet briar (*Rosa rubiginosa*), a prickly, perfumed wild rose often found in hedgerows.

24 June — bonfire

> Down by the shore the big Midsummer bonfire was lit, and all the people from the valley and the woods would gather to admire it. Other fires were lit further along the shore and out on the islands, but the Moomin Valley fire used to be the biggest. When the flames rose to their highest, Moomintroll used to wade out in the warm water and lie on his back floating on the swell and looking at the fire.

Today is the traditional midsummer's day and bonfires are lit at celebrations across Europe (including Moomin Valley), marking the zenith of the summer sun (though the actual solstice is two days earlier. It's if the blaze on the land answers the blaze in the heavens, but it also suggests the headlong craziness of summertime. The word bonfire has the more sinister root of bone fire – possibly linking the practice to sacrificial offerings. The Finnish title of Tove Jansson's *Moomin Summer Madness* – from which our quotation comes – means 'Dangerous Midsummer'. Watch out!

25 June

incalescence

Things are beginning to heat up in June, even in the British Isles – sweaters and coats will have been put away at the back of the wardrobe and T-shirts and shorts will be worn, come what may. When the temperature makes a leap and bound like this, you could try out the word 'incalescence' – a growing heat.

26 June

magpie

> One for sorrow,
> Two for mirth,
> Three for a wedding,
> Four for death.

The name of the magpie derives from the medieval habit of adding personal names to bird names (see 13 December – 'Robin'): here 'Mag' – the shortened form of Margaret – plus *pie*, from the Latin for magpie, *pica*.

The famous nursery rhyme reflects the superstitions generally attached to the crow family, seen as birds of ill-omen; the magpie, with its striking black-and-white plumage, is more ambivalent, promising both joy and sorrow. The rhyme comes in many versions, but this rather short and brutal one is one of the earliest recorded.

noonbeams

Stay, rivulet, nor haste to leave
  The lovely vale that lies around thee.
Why wouldst thou be a sea at eve,
  When but a fount the morning found thee?

Born when the skies began to glow,
  Humblest of all the rock's cold daughters,
No blossom bowed its stalk to show
  Where stole thy still and scanty waters.

Now on the stream the noonbeams look,
  Usurping, as thou downward driftest,
Its crystal from the clearest brook,
  Its rushing current from the swiftest.

Ah! what wild haste! – and all to be
  A river and expire in ocean.
Each fountain's tribute hurries thee
  To that vast grave with quicker motion.

Far better 'twere to linger still
  In this green vale, these flowers to cherish,
And die in peace, an aged rill,
  Than thus, a youthful Danube, perish.

– William Cullen Bryant

With its delightful play on moonbeam, William Cullen Bryant's translation of this Spanish poem by Pedro de Castro y Añaya celebrates and cautions the sun-kissed rivulet to make the most of its time as hastens through the landscape in its journey to the sea – a wise lesson for us all.

28 June

shinrin-yoku

Japan is two-thirds forest yet more than 90 per cent of its people are city dwellers. Getting out into nature, then, has become something of a health trend in recent years, encapsulated in the notion of *shinrin-yoku* – forest bathing – first coined in 1982. All that fresh air, all those oils and resins, all that space, have a deeply therapeutic effect. From Japan, forest bathing – sometimes billed as sylvotherapy – has caught on around the world.

29 June

stoggy

The low, five-note coo of the wood pigeon captures the essence of summer – gently lulling us to sleep as we laze beneath a tree. The Northumbrian or Yorkshire dialect word for the wood pigeon is a stoggy.

30 June

passerine

A beautiful word describing all perching birds (as well as all song-birds), encompassing everything from sparrows and tits to jays and crows. The word comes from the Latin for swallow, *passer*, which leads us nicely into July...

July

> The fervent heat, but so much more endurable in this pure air – the white and pink pond-blossoms, with great heart-shaped leaves; the glassy waters of the creek, the banks, with dense bushery, and the picturesque beeches and shade and turf; the tremulous, reedy call of some bird from recesses, breaking the warm, indolent, half-voluptuous silence; an occasional wasp, hornet, honey-bee or bumble [...] the vast space of the sky overhead so clear, and the buzzard up there sailing his slow whirl in majestic spirals and discs; just over the surface of the pond, two large slate-color'd dragon-flies, with wings of lace, circling and darting and occasionally balancing themselves quite still, their wings quivering all time.
>
> – Walt Whitman, 'A July Afternoon by the Pond'

Walt Whitman's passage, from his autobiographical collection of vignettes *Specimen Days*, gives us July in a woodland pond: the sweltering heat and the cooling shade, the vivid growth of flowers and the bees and wasps to feed on them, the indolence and near-frantic activity, and – above everything – the vast azure sky and the eyeball of the sun.

We will amble among many of these things in this month of words – half in a dream.

dayspring

Let's begin with the sun, our leitmotif for July:

> The sun had not yet risen. The sea was indistinguishable from the sky, except that the sea was slightly creased as if a cloth had wrinkles in it. Gradually as the sky whitened a dark line lay on the horizon dividing the sea from the sky and the grey cloth became barred with thick strokes moving, one after another, beneath the surface, following each other, pursuing each other, perpetually.
>
> As they neared the shore each bar rose, heaped itself, broke and swept a thin veil of white water across the sand. The wave paused, and then drew out again, sighing like a sleeper whose breath comes and goes unconsciously. Gradually the dark bar on the horizon became clear as if the sediment in an old wine-bottle had sunk and left the glass green. Behind it, too, the sky cleared as if the white sediment there had sunk, or as if the arm of a woman couched beneath the horizon had raised a lamp and flat bars of white, green and yellow spread across the sky like the blades of a fan. Then she raised her lamp higher and the air seemed to become fibrous and to tear away from the green surface flickering and flaming in red and yellow fibres like the smoky fire that roars from a bonfire. Gradually the fibres of the burning bonfire were fused into one haze, one incandescence which lifted the weight of the woollen grey sky on top of it and turned it to a million atoms of soft blue. The surface of the sea slowly became transparent and lay rippling and sparkling until the dark stripes were almost rubbed out. Slowly the arm that held the lamp raised it higher and then higher until a broad flame became visible; an arc of fire burnt on the rim of the horizon, and all round it the sea blazed gold.

Virginia Woolf's *The Waves* – perhaps the most experimental of her experimental novels – traces the lives of six people, from childhood through adulthood, weaving their voices together in successive 'waves', from sunrise to sunset. The book's opening comprises this lyrical depiction of a sunrise over the sea and the gradual intensification of light and its interaction with the water.

Of all the poetic alternatives for 'sunrise' – and there are many – a favourite is 'dayspring', first used in Middle English and often used for 'dawn', usually with religious overtones, in the King James Version of the Bible. Its blend of light and youthfulness seems just right for Woolf's description and the voices of the children playing in a garden we are about to meet.

2 JULY

dog days

> Sophia and Grandmother sat down by the shore to discuss the matter further. It was a pretty day, and the sea was running a long, windless swell. It was on days just like this – dog days – that boats went sailing off all by themselves. Large, alien objects made their way in from sea, certain things sank and others rose, milk soured, and dragonflies danced in desperation. Lizards were not afraid. When the moon came up, red spiders mated on uninhabited skerries, where the rock became an unbroken carpet of tiny, ecstatic spiders.

We are still by the sea, this time on an island somewhere in the Gulf of Finland. This passage – from Tove Jansson's adult novel *The Summer Book* – uses the term 'dog days'. Since ancient Greek times these have been the too hot days of summer, when things get feverish, a little crazy, and got their name from Sirius, the Dog Star, which rose in the night sky around this time. The original Swedish of Jansson's book uses the word *rötmånaden* – rot month.

3 July

thunder-plump

> Before we were well out of the Park, an even-down thunder-plump came on, that not only drookit the Doctor to the skin, but made my sky-blue silk clothes cling like wax to my skin.

It's not all sunshine in July, of course, and the close, stifling weather can cause sudden, heavy downpours of rain, with big stout drops – in Scotland and other regions sometimes known as a thunder-plump. Who knew you needed an umbrella in July? Still, after all this heat, we may be yearning for a drenching!

Scottish novelist John Galt's novel *The Steam-Boat*, published in 1822, provides the first recorded use.

4 July

halcyon

> All in the golden afternoon
> Full leisurely we glide;
> For both our oars, with little skill,
> By little arms are plied,
> While little hands make vain pretence
> Our wanderings to guide.
>
> Ah, cruel Three! In such an hour,
> Beneath such dreamy weather,
> To beg a tale of breath too weak
> To stir the tiniest feather!
> Yet what can one poor voice avail
> Against three tongues together?

The halcyon summer days of childhood are evoked in Lewis Carroll's introduction to *Alice's Adventures in Wonderland*. The book has its origin, Carroll claimed, in a 'golden afternoon' on 4 July 1862, spent boating and picnicking on the river Isis (a branch of the Thames) with the three Liddell sisters (including Alice Liddell – the Alice of the story). While rowing he entertained the children with his fantastic tales of Wonderland.

The word 'halcyon', denoting an idyllic time, comes from the Greek for kingfisher, and the birds' association with watery tranquility from the myth that the gods calmed the seas during their nesting season.

5 July

clockleddy

Ladybird, ladybird,
Fly away home,
Your house is on fire
And your children all gone;
All except one
And that's little Ann,
And she has crept under
The warming pan.

The ladybird (*Coccinella spp.*) is certainly the most welcome of our summer insects, its colourful, usually spotted wing cases (*elytra*) making it easily recognizable. The seven-spot ladybird (*Coccinella septempunctata*) with its black-spotted deep-red 'cloak' is the 'classic' of the genus, but there are plenty of other species and colours.

Human affection for the ladybird has helped give it many dialect names – it's a 'clockleddy' in Scotland, a 'ladycow' in Yorkshire, a 'bishy' in East Anglia, and, of course, a 'ladybug' in the US. It is also the leading lady in this well-known – bur rather tragic – nursery rhyme, a form of which was first recorded in the first half of the 18th century.

6 July — calefaction

A scientific, Latinate word for 'warming' or 'getting hotter'. For example, a garden pond undergoes calefaction in the summer months, which can cause stress to its wildlife. Experts advise covering the pond with a sail or similar to help keep the water cool and oxygenated.

7 July — smuir

Many people love the summer heat, but for others it can be stultifying, almost like a prison. The Scots have a word for this close weather – 'smuir' – which comes from the term to choke or smother and is equally well applied to sultry summer days.

bioluminescence

Once a dream did weave a shade
O'er my Angel-guarded bed,
That an Emmet lost it's way
Where on grass methought I lay.

Troubled, wildered and forlorn,
Dark benighted travel-worn,
Over many a tangled spray,
All heart-broke I heard her say:

'Oh my children! do they cry,
Do they hear their father sigh?
Now they look abroad to see,
Now return and weep for me.'

Pitying, I drop'd a tear:
But I saw a glow-worm near,
Who replied, 'What wailing wight
Calls the watchman of the night?

'I am set to light the ground,
While the beetle goes his round:
Follow now the beetle's hum;
Little wanderer, hie thee home!'

– William Blake, 'A Dream'

Despite their name, glow-worms (*Lampyris noctiluca*) are not worms, but beetles. In this poem by William Blake, these 'watchmen of the night' seem providential, guiding the lost ant – 'emmet' – home.

As with all glow-worms, it is only the wingless larvae and the adult females that are bioluminescent and which strictly therefore deserve the name (the winged males emit a little light).

lepidopterist

By universal suffrage, the place of highest rank among the butterflies of Britain has been accorded to this splendid insect, who merits his imperial title by reason of his robe of royal purple, the lofty throne he assumes, and the boldness and elevation of his flight.

A glimpse of this august personage on the wing is enough to fire the collector with enthusiastic ambition for his capture; sometimes a matter of the easiest accomplishment, sometimes just as hopelessly impossible, according to his majesty's humour of the moment.

Cowardice is not one of his attributes, and if he has formed a preference for any especial spot, he will risk loss of liberty and life rather than forsake it.

The Victorians loved butterflies but they also loved to catch and display them, as in this description of the treetop-flitting purple emperor (*Apatura iris*) – from the classic of 19th-century lepidoptery, *British Butterflies: Figures and Descriptions of Every Native Species*, by the painter and illustrator William Stephen Coleman. No middle-class home was complete without a mounted display of pinned and carefully captioned butterflies.

We may balk at the butterfly catching, but reading Coleman's gorgeous prose alongside his meticulous illustrations is a salutary experience, as it underscores the devasting diminishment of butterfly life that Britain has undergone in the last hundred years or more.

10 July

komorebi

A Japanese word for dappled sunlight dancing through leaves – a staple of haiku and woodblock prints. The English 'mogshade' (see 30 May) means the same thing but doesn't have quite the same cultural authenticity.

aurelian

From cocoon forth a butterfly
As lady from her door
Emerged – a summer afternoon –
Repairing everywhere,

Without design, that I could trace,
Except to stray abroad
On miscellaneous enterprise
The clovers understood.

Her pretty parasol be seen
Contracting in a field
Where men made hay, then struggling hard
With an opposing cloud,

Where parties, phantom as herself,
To Nowhere seemed to go
In purposeless circumference,
As 't were a tropic show.

And notwithstanding bee that worked,
And flower that zealous blew,
This audience of idleness
Disdained them, from the sky

Till sundown crept, a steady tide,
And men that made the hay,
And afternoon, and butterfly,
Extinguished in its sea.

– Emily Dickinson, 'The Butterfly's Day'

We have met lepidopterists a little earlier, but an even more archaic term for the study of butterflies and moths is aurelian. The word comes from the Latin for golden, *aureus*, referencing the golden colour of some chrysalises. Emily Dickinson imagines a butterfly emerging from its cocoon mirroring a lady stepping out for a summer's afternoon.

12 July

nightingale

Thou wast not born for death, immortal bird!
No hungry generations tread thee down;
The voice I hear this passing night was heard
In ancient days by emperor and clown:
Perhaps the self-same song that found a path
Through the sad heart of Ruth, when, sick for home,
She stood in tears amid the alien corn;
The same that oft-times hath
Charmed magic casements, opening on the foam
Of perilous seas, in fairy lands forlorn.

John Keats' ode 'To a Nightingale' includes what is perhaps the most famous stanza in Romantic poetry, in which the poet imagines people down the ages taking solace from the enduring song of the nightingale. The 'alien corn' and 'magic casements' are phrases that continue to resonate.

Despite the Romantic myth and its name – from the Old English *nihtegale*, 'night singer' – the (male) nightingale (*Luscinia megarhynchos*) sings both day and night as it seeks out a mate. Nonetheless, its clear-throated, high-pitched melody is best heard at dusk when there are fewer distracting noises.

foreglow

The dawn came. They stood together on a high place, an earthwork of the stone-age men, watching for the light. It came over the land. But the land was dark. She watched a pale rim on the sky, away against the darkened land. The darkness became bluer. A little wind was running in from the sea behind. It seemed to be running to the pale rift of the dawn. And she and he darkly, on an outpost of the darkness, stood watching for the dawn.

The light grew stronger, gushing up against the dark sapphire of the transparent night. The light grew stronger, whiter, then over it hovered a flush of rose. A flush of rose, and then yellow, pale, new-created yellow, the whole quivering and poising momentarily over the fountain on the sky's rim.

The rose hovered and quivered, burned, fused to flame, to a transient red, while the yellow urged out in great waves, thrown from the ever-increasing fountain, great waves of yellow flinging into the sky, scattering its spray over the darkness, which became bluer and bluer, paler, till soon it would itself be a radiance, which had been darkness.

The sun was coming. There was a quivering, a powerful terrifying swim of molten light. Then the molten source itself surged forth, revealing itself.

The rainbow may be the lemotif of D H Lawrence's novel of the same name, but other natural phenomena are used equally evocatively. Here Ursula and Skrebensky have a glorious vision of sunrise, but, bathed in the beauty of the foreglow, they end up reflecting on their own relationship.

holloway

I love at eventide to walk alone
Down narrow lanes o'erhung with dewy thorn
Where, from the long grass underneath, the snail
Jet-black creeps out and sprouts his timid horn
I love to muse o'er meadows newly mown
Where withering grass perfumes the sultry air
Where bees search round with sad and weary drone
In vain for flowers that bloomed but newly there
While in the juicey corn the hidden quail
Cries 'wet my foot' and, hid as thoughts unborn,
The fairy-like and seldom-seen land-rail
Utters 'craik craik' like voices underground
Right glad to meet the evening's dewy veil
And see the light fade into glooms around

Holloways – sunken lanes; a characteristic feature of southern England – are ancient footpaths, worn into the landscape by the passage of walkers, pilgrims and herd animals over the ages, often canopied by trees to form tunnels or 'hollow ways'. Walking along one, it is easy to imagine yourself taken back in time a few hundred years, following in the footsteps of poets such as John Clare, who captured his encounters with nature whilst walking along one such holloway in 'Summer Moods'.

15 JULY

umbrageous

> He sighed profoundly and flung himself – there was passion in his movements which deserves the word – on the earth at the foot of the oak tree. He loved, beneath all of this summer transiency, to feel the earth's spine beneath him; for such he took the hard root of the oak tree to be.

The wide, umbrella-like sound of the word 'umbrageous' – from Latin *umbra*, 'shade' – may make us think of the spreading branches of an oak – a running thread in Virginia Woolf's experimental novel *Orlando*.

16 JULY

yeoubi

Korean for a light rain that falls while the sun is shining, and meaning 'fox rain'. The association of foxes with rain is found in folklore around the world, including in Britain, where a sunshower is sometimes called a 'fox's wedding'.

17 JULY

bull-adder

> Today I saw the dragonfly
> Come from the wells where he did lie.
> An inner impulse rent the veil
> Of his old husk: from head to tail
> Came out clear plates of sapphire mail.
> He dried his wings: like gauze they grew;
> Thro' crofts and pastures wet with dew
> A living flash of light he flew.

With its metallic colours, clattering transparent wings, and long tail-like abdomen, the dragonfly provides one of the most startling, even otherworldly, sights (and sounds) of summer rivers and wetlands. Here, in this extract from 'The Two Voices', Alfred, Lord Tennyson captures, our sense of wonder when we encounter these extraordinary insects.

There are 36 species of dragonfly in the UK alone, including the ferocious emperor dragonfly (*Anax imperator*), which eats its insect prey during its acrobatic flights. No wonder the dragonfly got its name and the many variations on this snaky-dragonish theme found across the British and Irish Isles – as the Scots 'bull-adder' or the Cornish 'nader-margh', meaning the same thing.

18 July

sweet peas

Here are sweet peas, on tip-toe for a flight:
With wings of gentle flush o'er delicate white,
And taper fingers catching at all things,
To bind them all about with tiny rings.

In this little stanza, John Keats distils the essence of the sweet pea (*Lathyrus odoratus*), the most delicate and fragrant flower of summer gardens. Native to Sicily, Sardinia and the Aegean, they did not reach British shores until the 17th century and became a popular garden annual only in the 19th (Keats was describing something of a novelty). Because they are now so ubiquitous, it comes something as a shock that, in the wild, they are classified as critically endangered.

bee

I will arise and go now, and go to Innisfree,
And a small cabin build there, of clay and wattles made;
Nine bean-rows will I have there, a hive for the honey-bee,
And live alone in the bee-loud glade.

So begins William Butler Yeats' utopian poem 'The Lake Isle of Innisfree'. Since ancient times bees have been revered – if not always with strict zoological accuracy – as messengers of the gods, as hard, loyal workers and as models of community, even communistic, spirit. For Yeats, though, bees represent a desire for a life away from the grey city, the demands of society, and Ireland's troubled times – a life of freedom, independence and isolation.

As might be expected of such a key word, the monosyllabic 'bee' has kept much the same meaning since the Proto-Indo-European **bhei-* spoken on the Pontic–Caspian steppe five or so thousand years ago.

20 July

midge

Whence do ye come, ye creatures? Each of you
Is perfect as an angel! wings and eyes
Stupendous in their beauty – gorgeous dyes
In feathery fields of purple and of blue!
Would God I saw a moment as ye do!
I would become a molecule in size,
Rest with you, hum with you, or slanting rise
Along your one dear sunbeam, could I view
The pearly secret which each tiny fly –
Each tiny fly that hums and bobs and stirs
Hides in its little breast eternally
From you, ye prickly, grim philosophers
With all your theories that sound so high:
Hark to the buz a moment, my good sirs!

George MacDonald's poem 'On a Midge' casts an unusually friendly eye on these insects, clouds of which are considered the bane of the Scottish summer (if the country can be said to have such a season). Angels... really?

There are many species that are described as midges – essentially all tiny flies, or dipterans – but here the critter is the Highland midge (*Culicoides impunctatus*). 'Midge' is related to other European-language words for fly, such as German *Mücke* and Latin *musca*.

21 July

syke

A narrow stream, often not much more than a ditch, that often dries up in summer. Scan an Ordinance Survey map of Northumbria and you will find dozens of named sykes flowing down from the Cheviots.

azure

A something in a summer's day
As slow her flambeaux burn away,
Which solemnizes me.

A something in a summer's noon, –
A azure depth, a wordless tune,
Transcending ecstasy.

And still within a summer's night
A something so transporting bright,
I clap my hands to see;

Then veil my too inspecting face,
Lets such a subtle, shimmering grace
Flutter too far for me.

The wizard-fingers never rest,
The purple brook within the breast
Still chafes it narrow bed;

Still rears the East her amber flag,
Guides still the sun along the crag
His caravan of red,

Like flowers that heard the tale of dews,
But never deemed the dripping prize
Awaited their low brows

Or bees, that thought the summer's name
Some rumor of delirium
No summer could for them;

Or Arctic creature, dimly stirred
By tropic hint,—some travelled bird
Imported to the wood;

Or wind's bright signal to the ear,
Making that homely and severe,
Contented, known, before

The heaven unexpected came,
To lives that thought their worshipping
A too presumptuous psalm.

Azure is a rather hackneyed adjective for describing the clear blue of a summer's day – though not, of course, in Emily Dickinson's joyful poem 'Psalm of the Day'.

The word comes from the much-prized deep-blue rock lapis lazuli – from the Latin *lapis*, 'stone', plus the rock's Persian name *āžward*. Mined for millennia, it was ground to make the precious pigment ultramarine, used at great expense and for its wow factor in late medieval and Renaissance art. Titian's painting of *Bacchus and Ariadne*, in London's National Gallery, shows it off in a baking azure sky.

23 July

meriggiare

Meriggiare is the Italian for 'to rest in the shade during the midday heat' – ultimately from the Latin meridies, 'noon'. Italian Nobel Prize-winning poet Eugenio Montale's poem begins '*Meriggiare pallido e assorto*' (Noonday slumber, pallid and rapt) – evoking a summer's day spent relaxing in a shady hillside garden in Umbria.

24 July — rindle

Imagine you are lying beside a stream on a hot summer's day. In among the birdsong you can hear the faint trickle of the water, the flow much reduced by the heat and lack of rain: rindle describes both the flow and sound of that babbling water course. Soon you are dozing and your gentle snores join the summer music.

25 July — meridional

Warm summer sun,
  Shine kindly here,
Warm southern wind,
  Blow softly here.
Green sod above,
  Lie light, lie light.
Good night, dear heart,
  Good night, good night.

This simple summer lullaby, 'Warm Summer Sun', was adapted by Mark Twain from a poem by the Australian poet Robert Richardson and used as an epitaph for his daughter Susy, who died in 1896.

We're in the Goldilocks zone – neither cold nor too hot, but just right. Meridional refers to the sunny south of a country, especially of France.

26 July

flea

It's unnerving that, in summer, fleas can lay as many as 50 eggs a day, and that the next generation will be laying their own a fortnight later. Even more unnerving that there is an enduring tradition, dating back to ancient times, of love poems involving fleas in a rather saucy way. John Donne's 'The Flea' is by far the most famous of these:

> Mark but this flea, and mark in this,
> How little that which thou deniest me is;
> It sucked me first, and now sucks thee,
> And in this flea our two bloods mingled be;
> Thou know'st that this cannot be said
> A sin, nor shame, nor loss of maidenhead,
> Yet this enjoys before it woo,
> And pampered swells with one blood made of two,
> And this, alas, is more than we would do.

Take heart from the fact that Donne's flea – the so-called human flea (*Pulex irritans*), now known to have been a vector in the transmission of the plague bacterium, *Yersinia pestis* – is now rarely found in homes.

27 July

leesome

A Scots word for a fine summer's day – use it while you can.

peach

Would you like to throw a stone at me?
Here, take all that's left of my peach.

Blood-red, deep:
Heaven knows how it came to pass.
Somebody's pound of flesh rendered up.

Wrinkled with secrets
And hard with the intention to keep them.

Why, from silvery peach-bloom,
From that shallow-silvery wine-glass on a short stem
This rolling, dropping, heavy globule?

I am thinking, of course, of the peach before I ate it.

Why so velvety, why so voluptuous heavy?
Why hanging with such inordinate weight?
Why so indented?
Why the groove?
Why the lovely, bivalve roundnesses?
Why the ripple down the sphere?
Why the suggestion of incision?

Why was not my peach round and finished like a billiard ball?
It would have been if man had made it.
Though I've eaten it now.

But it wasn't round and finished like a billiard ball;
And because I say so, you would like to throw something at me.

Here, you can have my peach stone.

We rarely think of D H Lawrence as humorous but here, in 'Peach', he is brilliantly and offhandedly so, as he contemplates his half-eaten peach and the infuriation of, we assume, his wife, Frieda (he must have been annoying at times). Funnily enough, or not, the word derives from the Latin *Persicum malum* – Persian apple.

29 July

tyger

Tyger Tyger, burning bright,
In the forests of the night;
What immortal hand or eye,
Could frame thy fearful symmetry?

In what distant deeps or skies.
Burnt the fire of thine eyes?
On what wings dare he aspire?
What the hand, dare seize the fire?

And what shoulder, & what art,
Could twist the sinews of thy heart?
And when thy heart began to beat.
What dread hand? & what dread feet?

What the hammer? what the chain,
In what furnace was thy brain?
What the anvil? what dread grasp.
Dare its deadly terrors clasp?

When the stars threw down their spears
And water'd heaven with their tears:
Did he smile his work to see?
Did he who made the Lamb make thee?

Tyger Tyger burning bright,
In the forests of the night:
What immortal hand or eye,
Dare frame thy fearful symmetry?

The 29th July is Global Tiger Day – a day dedicated to celebrating these magnificent creatures and raising awareness of the threats to tigers in the wild. Poet and printmaker William Blake chose to showcase the tiger as the ultimate symbol of wildness and ferocity in his much-loved poem – drawing the contrast between it and the lamb as metaphors for the balance of ferocity and mildness, or innocence and experience, inherent to all creation. The word tiger, ultimately derives from a Proto-Indo-European root **(s)teyg-* or sharp.

30 July

chelonian

You know what it is to be born alone,
Baby tortoise!

The first day to heave your feet little by little from
  the shell,
Not yet awake,
And remain lapsed on earth,
Not quite alive.

A tiny, fragile, half-animate bean.

To open your tiny beak-mouth, that looks as if it would
  never open,
Like some iron door;
To lift the upper hawk-beak from the lower base
And reach your skinny little neck
And take your first bite at some dim bit of herbage,
Alone, small insect,
Tiny bright-eye,
Slow one.

D H Lawrence's poems about animals and flowers are charged with empathetic insight as well as natural vitality, as in his 'Baby Tortoise'. Lawrence watched tortoises closely while staying in a villa in Tuscany, Italy, and devoted a six-poem collection, *Tortoises*, to the 'slow ones' – for him, symbols of instinctual, bodily life.

Etymologists debate the origins of the lugubrious-sounding word 'tortoise'. Does it come from Latin *tortus*, 'twisted', referring to those short, stubby legs? Or, more abstrusely, is somehow a distortion of Tartaros, the deepest part of the Underworld in Greek mythology. The latter seems unlikely since the ancient Greeks had a perfect good word for a tortoise or turtle, *khelṓnē*, which turns up in the order adjective, chelonian.

31 JULY

heliophilous

> I'm painting with the gusto of a Marseillais eating bouillabaisse, which won't surprise you when it's a question of painting large Sunflowers. I have 3 canvases on the go. [...] I'll probably not stop there. In the hope of living in a studio of our own with Gauguin, I'd like to do a decoration for the studio. Nothing but large Sunflowers.

So wrote Vincent van Gogh to his brother Theo in the summer of 1888. For Van Gogh, the sunflower (*Helianthus annuus*) – *tournesol* in French – was the embodiment of vitality, optimism, generosity, gratitude... of life itself, and he painted them near obsessively, both in Paris and most especially during his stay in the South. Sunflowers are famously 'heliophilous', or sun-loving – a quality, often, of the holidaying nature lovers whom we will come across next month...

August

Live in the sunshine, swim the sea.
Drink in the wild air's salubrity.

– Ralph Waldo Emerson, 'Merlin's Song'

Summer has grown tall enough to tip over into autumn...but not quite yet. Many trees and flowers are at their very peak, and every hedgerow, every wood, is an inextricable tangle of growing things. The weather, too, is holding steady – days are more likely warm, dry and sunny than not. Nonetheless, there is a timbre of dusty exhaustion about the world – the fresh green of early summer has long since passed away.

But let's not talk the month down – for us humans it's holiday season, so in this month's words we'll spend more time at the beach, go up to the Scottish Highlands, and even to the south of France. Wherever we are, let's take Emerson's advice.

1 August

Lughnasa

ROSE (Quietly, resolutely.) It was last Sunday week, the first night of the Festival of Lughansa; and they were doing what they do every year up there in the back hills.

KATE. Festival of Lughnasa! What sort of –

ROSE. First they light a bonfire beside a spring well. Then they dance round it. Then they drive their cattle through the flames to banish the devil out of them.

Lughnasa, held on 1 August, was an old Gaelic celebration, marking the beginning of the harvest season and including feasting, bonfires and offerings of first fruits to the god Lugh. It has lingered on in some rural communities, as in the County Donegal of Brian Friel's play *Dancing at Lughnasa*, set in the 1930s. It involved a pilgrimage into the 'back hills' and wild dancing, oftentimes condemned as pagan revelry by the Church. For the play's five unmarried Mundy sisters, the dancing represents a joyful outpouring of bodily and spiritual freedom and a return to nature.

Lammas (*hlāfmæsse*) is a Christianized Anglo-Saxon equivalent, meaning 'Loaf Mass', when local people gave a loaf as an offering in the parish church.

2 August **dingle**

A lovely word for a wooded valley or hollow, though in origin it related to the Old English words for 'pit' and 'dungeon'. It takes a starring role in the first stanza of Dylan Thomas' summery poem 'Fern Hill':

> Now as I was young and easy under the apple boughs
> About the lilting house and happy as the grass was green,
> The night above the dingle starry,
> Time let me hail and climb
> Golden in the heydays of his eyes,
> And honoured among wagons I was prince of the apple towns
> And once below a time I lordly had the trees and leaves
> Trail with daisies and barley
> Down the rivers of the windfall light.

3 August **cerulean**

Hopefully an adjective for the sky when you are away on your holidays – from the Latin for sky blue, *caeruleus*.

4 August **woad**

In Latin, the original name of the month was *Sextilis mensi* – the sixth month in the Roman calendar – but it was renamed *Augustus mensi* in honour of the first emperor, Augustus Caesar. The Anglo-Saxons cut the month back to size: St Bede tells us in his *The Reckoning of Time* that they called August *Wēodmōnaþ*, or 'Weed Month'. *Wēod* in Old English referred to any plant, both useful ones (specifically, woad – source of a blue dye) and unwanted ones, what we call 'weeds'. So the month's name merely suggested the rampant growth of late summer. Curiously, *augustus*, too, has the implication of abundance, as it seems to derive from the Latin verb *augere*, 'to grow'.

5 August

mordros

A Cornish word for the sound of the sea (*mor*, meaning sea, plus *dros*, sound). The word appears in several Cornish seaside or clifftop place names, such as Morvah or Morwenstow, where the roar of the Atlantic is never far from your ears.

6 August

hoglet

The hedgehog hides beneath the rotten hedge
And makes a great round nest of grass and sedge,
Or in a bush or in a hollow tree;
And many often stoop and say they see
Him roll and fill his prickles full of crabs
And creep away; and where the magpie dabs
His wing at muddy dyke, in aged root
He makes a nest and fills it full of fruit,
On the hedge bottom hunts for crabs and sloes
And whistles like a cricket as he goes.
It rolls up like a ball or shapeless hog
When gipsies hunt it with their noisy dog;
I've seen it in their camps – they call it sweet,
Though black and bitter and unsavoury meat.

Summer is the most active time for the hedgehog, as it builds nests and raises its young, as here in John Clare's lovely poem 'The Hedgehog'. Clare's poems are often carefully built up from clear-eyed, unsentimental observations: we really get the picture here of the Northamptonshire poet crouching down beside a tangled hedgerow and examining the nest from close-up, perhaps with the four or five hoglets that are the typical hedgehog litter size. Hedgehogs will often have a first litter in June and a second, say, in August.

grassy

The grass so little has to do,—
A sphere of simple green,
With only butterflies to brood,
And bees to entertain,

And stir all day to pretty tunes
The breezes fetch along,
And hold the sunshine in its lap
And bow to everything;

And thread the dews all night, like pearls,
And make myself so fine,—
A duchess were too common
For such a noticing.

And even when it dies, to pass
In odors so divine,
As lowly spices gone to sleep,
Or amulets of pine

And then to dwell in sovereign barns,
And dream the days away,—
The grass so little has to do,
I wish I were the hay!

– Emily Dickinson, 'The Grass'

There are still some nature words that need to be coined. The smell of new-cut grass is often cited as a favourite odour, evoking memories of childhood and lazy afternoons in the sun, but somehow there is no word other than grassy for this beloved scent. The best scientists can coin is GLV – the term for the green leaf volatile compounds that some plants emit to deter predators. Maybe we should take a leaf from petrichor on 13 May and coin 'herbichor' for this nostalgic smell.

8 August

spoondrift

> Some of the scenes thus revealed were of immeasurable grandeur and of absorbing interest – the sea, running mountains high, threw skywards with each wave mighty masses of white foam, which the tempest seemed to snatch at and whirl away into space; here and there a fishing-boat, with a rag of sail, running madly for shelter before the blast; now and again the white wings of a storm-tossed sea-bird.
>
> – Bram Stoker, *Dracula*

Bram Stoker's account of the storm on this day that brought the ill-fated schooner the *Demeter*, and with it Dracula, to Whitby, was based on a real life 'storm of great violence' and the stranding of the *Dmitry* in 1885. The power of the waves in both cases drew onlookers, who doubtless would have been soaked by the 'spoondrift' – a Scots word for the spray blown from cresting waves during a gale.

9 August

marlie

On Shetland, the waters of sheltered narrow sea inlets, locally called voes, are sometimes home to underwater forests of common eelgrass (*Zostera marina*) – which is a flowering plant rather than a seaweed. They provide a vital ecosystem, nurseries to young cod and plaice, home to cuttlefish and mud snails, and, when exposed, fodder for birds like brent geese. The local name is marlie or marlok, likely from the Old Norse *marlauk*, meaning 'sea onion' (they do look a little like swaying underwater spring onions!).

canicular

> There was the same red glare as far as eye could reach, and small waves were lapping the hot sand in little, flurried gasps. As I slowly walked toward the boulders at the end of the beach I could feel my temples swelling under the impact of the light. It pressed itself on me, trying to check my progress. And each time I felt a hot blast strike my forehead, I gritted my teeth, I clenched my fists in my trouser pockets and keyed up every nerve to fend off the sun and the dark befuddlement it was pouring into me. Whenever a blade of vivid light shot upward from a bit of shell or broken glass lying on the sand, my jaws set hard. I wasn't going to be beaten, and I walked steadily on.

Heat waves – periods of extreme heat outside the normal weather pattern – can be disastrous – for human and animal health and well-being. They can threaten crops and trigger destructive wildfires. They are becoming increasingly common and intense, as the planet dangerously warms. The French word for a heat wave is *canicule*, and canicular, describing periods of intense heat, exists in English, too. Both derive from the Latin *canicular*, 'little dog', and relate to the dog days of summer (see 2 July).

One of the most powerful descriptions of extreme heat and its effects on humans is in Albert Camus' existentialist novel *L'Étranger* (The Stranger or The Outsider), about a *pied-noir* (French colonial inhabitant of Algeria) who kills an Arab Algerian 'because of the burning sun', as he later claims.

Summer can be a violent season as well as a wonderful one.

11 August — luminescence

> There was a bright full moon, with heavy black, driving clouds, which threw the whole scene into a fleeting diorama of light and shade as they sailed across. For a moment or two I could see nothing, as the shadow of a cloud obscured St Mary's Church and all around it. Then as the cloud passed I could see the ruins of the abbey coming into view; and as the edge of a narrow band of light as sharp as a sword-cut moved along, the church and the churchyard became gradually visible.

Of course, not all seaside holidays are sun-kissed. Here Mina Murray – soon to become Mrs Mina Harker – journals her experience on this night in Whitby. She sees the remains of the abbey bathed by the luminescence of the moon, and her friend Lucy Westenra with a dark figure behind her, before the scene is obscured by a cloud, setting off the chain of events events that follow the arrival in England of Dracula in Bram Stoker's gothic novel.

12 August — grouse

> Yon wild mossy mountains sae lofty and wide,
> That nurse in their bosom the youth o' the Clyde,
> Where the grouse lead their coveys thro' the heather to feed,
> And the shepherd tends his flock as he pipes on his reed.

The so-called Glorious Twelfth marks the beginning of the grouse shooting season in Britain, the particular game species here being the red grouse (*Lagopus scotica*). The red grouse inhabits heather moorlands, such as those found abundantly in the Highlands of Scotland. Nowhere better, then, to find a depiction of the grouse and grouse-moors than in the work of Robert Burns, who in 'Yon Wild Mossy Mountains' turns the Grampians into a kind of chilly northern Arcadia.

For heather (ling) see 13 August, and for moss, 19 August.

ling

Lower on the mountain, on all the slopes and shoulders and ridges and on the moors below, the characteristic growth is heather. And this too is integral to the mountain. For heather grows in its most profuse luxuriance on granite, so that the very substance of the mountain is in its life. Of the three varieties that grow on these hills – two Ericas and the ling – the July-blooming bell heather is the least beautiful, though its clumps of hot red are like sun-bursts when the rest of the hills are still brown. The pale cross-leaved heath, that grows in small patches, often only single heads, in moist places, is an exquisite, almost waxen-still, with a honey perfume.

But it is the August-blooming ling that covers the hills with amethyst. Now they look gracious and benign. For many many miles there is nothing but this soft radiance. Walk over it in a hot sun, preferably not on a path ('I like the unpath best,' one of my small friends said when her father had called her to heel), and the scent rises in a heady cloud.

Nan Shepherd's sensual description of walking across heather comes from her great paean to hill-walking in the Grampians, *The Living Mountain* (for which, see also 11 May). No beaten track for her, but straight through the tough and tangled masses of low-growing *Calluna vulgaris* – the 'unpath' as she refers to it. Ling can refer to several moorland plant species but especially to common heather, and comes from Old Norse, perhaps with deeper origins in a word for 'unused land'.

14 August

cachalot

> This proud tosser of the waves has another and still more wonderful trait. When hunger plagues him on the deep, and the monster longs for food, this haunter of the sea opens his mouth, and sets his lips agape; whereupon there issues a ravishing perfume from his inwards, by which other kinds of fish are beguiled.
>
> With lively motions they swim to where the sweet odour comes forth, and there enter in, a heedless host, until the wide gorge is full; then, in one instant, he snaps his fierce jaws together about the swarming prey.

Regardless of the zoological inaccuracy, this excerpt from the 10th-century Anglo-Saxon poem 'The Whale' captures the awful grandeur of the sperm whale (*Physeter macrocephalus*) and provides us with some wonderful kennings: 'tosser of the waves' and 'haunter of the sea'. While the sperm whale is a pelagic (deep-ocean) mammal, it sometimes veers closer to shore and can even become stranded. Since the 18th century it has sometimes been known as the cachalot, from the Portuguese for 'big head'. Old tales of sailors casting anchor on whale backs, as found in the Anglo-Saxon poem, are of course fictitious – at least we hope so!

15 August

swash

The uprush of a wave on a beach. Watch out or you'll have sodden shoes and socks – along with a sand-speckled sandwich, one of the few unpleasant experiences of spending time on a beach.

16 AUGUST

cricket

Not the summertime sport, but the insects, which in the UK are at their busiest and loudest in August. In the British and Irish Isles what we loosely call crickets are mostly bush-crickets of various species such as the great green (*Tettigonia viridissima*) and the speckled (*Leptophyes punctatissima*). Sport and insect have different etymological origins: the sport likely from the Old English cricc, meaning a stick; the insect from *criquer*, Old French for 'to creak'. They can both, though, make a racket on hot summer afternoons.

17 AUGUST

verdure

> It was like a glimpse of Paradise to eyes fresh from autumnal grays and glooms, as they sped along the lovely coast, every curve and turn showing new combinations of sea and shore, olive-crowned cliff and shining mountain-peak. With every mile the blue became bluer, the wind softer, the feathery verdure more dense and summer-like. Hyères and Cannes and Antibes were passed, and then, as they rounded a long point, came the view of a sunshiny city lying on a sunlit shore; the train slackened its speed, and they knew that their journey's end was come and they were in Nice.

One of the highlights of a foreign holiday must surely be the first view of a sun-kissed destination: an exotic foreign city nestled in a bay, ringed by the lush green of fresh foreign verdure. In Susan Coolidge's novel *What Katy Did Next*, her irrepressible heroine travels to the south of France – a refreshing change from the drab streets of London and her home state of Ohio.

18 August **kea**

Across Cornwall, but especially at the very westerly end of the county, in Penwith, the tightly packed fields are bounded by earthen walls lined with granite intermingled with gorse and myriad flowers. Some of these date to Neolithic times and are home to countless species of insects and small animals. The Cornish word for these earth-and-stone hedges is a kea.

19 August **moss**

> More delicately, more intricately fashioned than any grasses of the field, more subtle in texture than any seaweed of the sea, more thickly woven, and with a sort of intimate passionate patience, by the creative spirit within it, than any forest leaves or any lichen upon any tree trunk, this sacred moss of Somersetshire would remain as a perfectly satisfying symbol of life if all other vegetation were destroyed out of that country. There is a religious reticence in the nature of moss.

John Cowper Powys is one of the greatest, but most overlooked, British novelists of the 20th century – a 'Dostoyevsky with teacups', as writer Margaret Drabble, described him. His ecstatic descriptions of nature in the West Country and his native Wales – as in this of moss in *A Glastonbury Romance* – find grandeur and a spiritual dimension in even the smallest organisms. Even in the heat of summer, moss still grows luxuriantly in damp, shady woods and about rivers. Elsewhere, a short burst of summer rain is enough to revive the tiny leaf-like structures – phyllids – of dried-out and seemingly dead moss.

20 August

hollyhock

> Deep red hollyhocks pressed against the limestone wall and velvet butterflies flopped lazily from flower to flower. It was Tennyson weather, drowsy, warm, unnaturally still.

L P Hartley's novel *The Go-Between* is the story of a boy who unwittingly becomes involved in a secret love affair between a squire's daughter and a tenant farmer. It is also one of the classic depictions of an English summer, albeit one with a dark underbelly of secrets and betrayal. Even the deep-red hollyhocks here seem to reek of something more than the flower per se – a staple of the cottage garden. The hollyhock (*Alcea* spp., in the mallow family) – an introducee from China in late medieval times – is the 'holy-mallow', prized for its medicinal properties.

21 August

fluctivagant

On a beach trip, you've thrown your dog's ball too far out into the sea so that even he daren't swim out to get it. Both you and he stand at the surf's edge and forlornly watch it bobbing up and down on the water's surface. To keep yourself from being too sad, you recall the word for an item floating in the sea – 'fluctivagant' – coined in a 17th-century dictionary by Elisha Coles. You mention it to your dog but he doesn't understand you... For more beach words, see 23 August.

22 August

smeuse

An English dialect word for a hole in a hedge made by the frequent passage of animals, such as a sheep, hare or rabbit. Its earliest recorded use is in the early 19th century, and it seems to be a portmanteau of two much older words: 'smoot', meaning small gap, and 'meuse', meaning winding path.

fluctisonant

The sea is calm tonight.
The tide is full, the moon lies fair
Upon the straits; on the French coast the light
Gleams and is gone; the cliffs of England stand,
Glimmering and vast, out in the tranquil bay.
Come to the window, sweet is the night-air!
Only, from the long line of spray
Where the sea meets the moon-blanched land,
Listen! you hear the grating roar
Of pebbles which the waves draw back, and fling,
At their return, up the high strand,
Begin, and cease, and then again begin,
With tremulous cadence slow, and bring
The eternal note of sadness in.

Sophocles long ago
Heard it on the Ægean, and it brought
Into his mind the turbid ebb and flow
Of human misery; we
Find also in the sound a thought,
Hearing it by this distant northern sea.

The Sea of Faith
Was once, too, at the full, and round earth's shore
Lay like the folds of a bright girdle furled.
But now I only hear
Its melancholy, long, withdrawing roar,
Retreating, to the breath
Of the night-wind, down the vast edges drear
And naked shingles of the world.

Ah, love, let us be true
To one another! for the world, which seems
To lie before us like a land of dreams,
So various, so beautiful, so new,
Hath really neither joy, nor love, nor light,
Nor certitude, nor peace, nor help for pain;
And we are here as on a darkling plain
Swept with confused alarms of struggle and flight,
Where ignorant armies clash by night.

Most of us who have stood on a beach on a summer's night will recognize the lonely roar of waves (fluctisonant) that are the leitmotif of Matthew Arnold's 'Dover Beach', published in 1867 but written much earlier in 1851, during his honeymoon. For Arnold, the melancholic sound of the 'withdrawing roar' as the tide retreats is a metaphor for the decline of Christian faith, characteristic (at least for some) of the Victorian era.

24 August

bumblekites

In his poem 'Blackberry-Picking', Seamus Heaney describes one of the great childhood pleasures – blackberrying – evocatively describing the sweet juices as like thickened wine 'summer's blood was in it'. It is just too hard not to eat any while you pick, even though you know you won't get away with your 'crime' because your mouth and hands will be stained with deep-purple juice.

Blackberries have all sorts of alternative names: 'brambles' (from Old English *bremel*), the Scottish scaldberries, 'wait-a-bits' (oh, but you just can't!) and the wonderful 'bumblekites' are just a few. They aren't true berries but clumps of tiny fruits, or dupelets.

Do try to keep some back for that crumble or cobbler!

anthophilous

Like trains of cars on tracks of plush
I hear the level bee:
A jar across the flowers goes,
Their velvet masonry

Withstands until the sweet assault
Their chivalry consumes,
While he, victorious, tilts away
To vanquish other blooms.

His feet are shod with gauze,
His helmet is of gold;
His breast, a single onyx
With chrysoprase, inlaid.

His labor is a chant,
His idleness a tune;
Oh, for a bee's experience
Of clovers and of noon!

– Emily Dickinson, 'The Bee'

Working in a garden, surrounded by flowers and the buzz of insects, is one of the best ways to spend a summer's afternoon. The flower lovers among us might describe themselves as anthophiles – from the Greek *antho-* meaning flower and *-philia* or loving – although the word is more often used to describe anthophilous insects, such as the busy bee of Emily Dickinson's short poem.

26 August

nectarine

What wond'rous life in this I lead!
Ripe apples drop about my head;
The luscious clusters of the vine
Upon my mouth do crush their wine;
The nectarine and curious peach
Into my hands themselves do reach;
Stumbling on melons as I pass,
Ensnar'd with flow'rs, I fall on grass.

We might think nectarine – a smooth-skinned variety of peach (*Prunus persica*) – is a newfangled fruit name invented by some canny marketer, but in fact it was coined as early as the 17th century (from *nectar* – food of the gods – plus *-ine*). One of its early uses is in the Metaphysical poet Andrew Marvell's 'The Garden'. The very word has a lusciously Edenic quality and here is used, among others mouthwatering fruits, as a temptation that precedes a fall.

27 August

flipperling

Oh! hush thee, my baby, the night is behind us,
And black are the waters that sparkled so green.
The moon, o'er the combers, looks downward to find us
At rest in the hollows that rustle between.
Where billow meets billow, there soft be thy pillow;
Ah, weary wee flipperling, curl at thy ease!
The storm shall not wake thee, nor shark overtake thee,
Asleep in the arms of the slow-swinging seas.

Rudyard Kipling's 'Seal Lullaby' (from *The Jungle Book*) uses a charming word for a seal pup – a flipperling. Late August is when the grey seal (*Halichoerus grypus*) begins to pup.

28 August — ambergris

Ambergris is a hard, waxy byproduct of the squid-rich diet of sperm whales, formed in their intestines and then vomited to float on the ocean. 'Yuck' is one's inevitable reaction, but over time its rank smell ages into sweet, earthy mustiness, making it highly prized by the perfume industry. Small amounts can fetch incredible prices, hence its moniker 'floating gold'. In 2016 a 2.7kg (6lb) lump of ambergris was washed up on a Lancashire beach and subsequently sold for £100,000.

The word itself, rather euphemistically, means 'grey amber'. Scour those beaches at holiday time!

29 August — humblebee

Burly dozing humblebee!
Where thou art is clime for me.
Let them sail for Porto Rique,
Far-off heats through seas to seek,
I will follow thee alone,
Thou animated torrid zone!
Zig-zag steerer, desert-cheerer,
Let me chase thy waving lines,
Keep me nearer, me thy hearer,
Singing over shrubs and vines.

– Ralph Waldo Emerson, 'The Humble Bee'

The buzz of busy bumblebees is one of the hallmarks of late summer as the insects make the most of the last of the flowers. Humblebee was once the common name for the creatures – evoking the hum of their wings – before it was overtaken by bumblebee, from a root meaning to drone or buzz.

30 August — minifer

Stoats (*Mustela erminea*) are much in evidence in August, as the kits leave their mothers and hunt for themselves. As yet, they still wear their brown summer coats, with white belly and black-tipped tail. Only in autumn proper will they turn pure white, (see 22 January), their fur – ermine – historically making them quarry for hunters.

In Scots, they were known as whitrets, 'white rats'; in East Anglia, minifers. The word 'stoat' itself is related to 'stout', meaning bold or brave – they are fierce hunters themselves.

Let's take care when we go traipsing through the wild wood...

31 August — rowan

> The Water Rat was restless, and he did not exactly know why. To all appearance the summer's pomp was still at fullest height, and although in the tilled acres green had given way to gold, though rowans were reddening, and the woods were dashed here and there with a tawny fierceness, yet light and warmth and colour were still present in undiminished measure, clean of any chilly premonitions of the passing year. But the constant chorus of the orchards and hedges had shrunk to a casual evensong from a few yet unwearied performers; the robin was beginning to assert himself once more; and there was a feeling in the air of change and departure.

Is it summer still, or has autumn come? Ratty wonders in Kenneth Grahame's novel *The Wind in the Willows*. The rowan (*Sorbus* spp.; see 28 May), with its bright-red berries, is one of the bellwethers here, but he is getting mixed messages. The blurriness of summer to autumn will be a theme of September...

September

Season of mists and mellow fruitfulness

– John Keats, 'To Autumn'

Come the first day of September and the first line of John Keats' ode 'To Autumn' is on the tip of many of our tongues, even if hardly a leaf has turned or, still less, fallen and the summer weather continues to be (if we're lucky) glorious. Perhaps only two or three weeks later does this Keatsian autumn really set in: our apple trees heave, mists dutifully gather on riverbanks, and wood smoke rises from country cottages as a nip creeps into the still-light evenings. Some melancholy types even claim to like autumn better than spring.

The last part of September sees the harvest proper, too – thick fields are shorn to stubble, turning arable land from gold to a rich tawny brown. Harvest Festival comes towards the very end of the month (or even at the beginning of October). Perhaps there's something in those melancholics' claims after all, and we can concur with one of the characters in F Scott Fitzgerald's *The Great Gatsby*: 'Life starts all over again when it gets crisp in the fall.'

1 SEPTEMBER

meander

Five miles meandering with a mazy motion
Through wood and dale the sacred river ran,
Then reached the caverns measureless to man,
And sank in tumult to a lifeless ocean;
And 'mid this tumult Kubla heard from far
Ancestral voices prophesying war!

The winding path of a river, a meander, is a gentle, lazy word, evoking an idyllic or dreamlike scene, so perhaps it is appropriate for a poem composed in a dream. The story attached to Samuel Taylor Coleridge's 'Kubla Kahn' is that the poet was walking near Nether Stowey and stopped to rest. There he had the dream which inspired the poem, but his peace was shattered by 'a man on business from Porlock', driving the majority of the composition from his mind.

aestivo-autumnal

> In plain common-place matter-of-fact, then, it was a fine morning – so fine that you would scarcely have believed that the few months of an English summer had yet flown by. Hedges, fields, and trees, hill and moorland, presented to the eye their ever-varying shades of deep rich green; scarce a leaf had fallen, scarce a sprinkle of yellow mingled with the hues of summer warned you that autumn had begun. The sky was cloudless, the sun shone out bright and warm; the songs of birds, and hum of myriads of summer insects, filled the air; and the cottage gardens, crowded with flowers of every rich and beautiful tint, sparkled, in the heavy dew, like beds of glittering jewels. Everything bore the stamp of summer, and none of its beautiful colours had yet faded from the dye.

There is, of course, no abrupt change from summer to autumn, or, indeed, from August to September, as here described in a hunt scene from Charles Dickens' *The Pickwick Papers*, set at the beginning of September. To all intents and purposes, summer lingers on; there are only a few subtle hints – a fallen leaf, a yellow patch of foliage – that things are changing. We might have turned to the term 'aestivo-autumnal' to describe the situation – only its use is confined to a severe form of malaria occurring at the very brink of late summer.

halig-monaþ

Mown meadows skirt the standing wheat;
I linger, for the hay is sweet,
New-cut and curing in the sun.
Like furrows, straight, the windrows run,
Fallen, gallant ranks that tossed and bent
When, yesterday, the west wind went
A-rioting through grass and grain.
To-day no least breath stirs the plain;
Only the hot air, quivering, yields
Illusive motion to the fields
Where not the slenderest tassel swings.
Across the wheat flash sky-blue wings;
A goldfinch dangles from a tall,
Full-flowered yellow mullein; all
The world seems turning blue and gold.
Unstartled, since, even from of old,
Beauty has brought keen sense of her,
I feel the withering grasses stir;
Along the edges of the wheat,
I hear the rustle of her feet:
And yet I know the whole sea lies,
And half the earth, between our eyes.

– Sophie Jewett, 'In Harvest'

The Old English name for September was *halig-monaþ*, 'holy month', or sometimes *hærfestmonað*, 'harvest month'. Both referred to the God-given bounty of the season.

4 SEPTEMBER

serotinal

From the Latin *serotinus*, 'late', serotinal is most often applied to flowers or insects that bloom or hatch at the end of summer, on the cusp of autumn. As we humans grow older, the more optimistic among us might like to think of ourselves as being serotinal, too – late bloomers.

5 SEPTEMBER

moonglade

> There is no Americanism more graceful than the word 'moonglade'. It is applied along our New England coast to that path of light which lies beneath the moon upon the sea, and which appears to slope down from the horizon to the place where each observer stands. This broad and luminous track is as distinct from the expanse around it as is any path through the forest from the surrounding trees; and both alike offer a vista for the imagination as well as a delight to the eye.
>
> – Thomas Wentworth Higginson, 'A Moonglade'

The full moon hanging low over a still body of water casts an avenue of light called a moonglade. Thomas Wentworth Higginson, prominent abolitionist and mentor to Emily Dickinson, described it as a broad and luminous track of light, and fancied it as the home of water wraiths, mermaids and the lingering fairies who own Ariel's sway.

6 SEPTEMBER

melancholy

> I love the autumn – that melancholy season that suits memories so well. When the trees have lost their leaves, when the sky at sunset still preserves the russet hue that fills with gold the withered grass, it is sweet to watch the final fading of the fires that until recently burnt within you.
>
> – Gustave Flaubert, *November*

Autumn is beautiful, and made more so in the consciousness that it will soon pass. Melancholy – pensive sadness – is the season's badge.

7 SEPTEMBER

conker

> I have always loved this month. As a school boy I loved it because it is the Month of the Conker. It is no good knocking down conkers in August because they are still soft and white. But in September, ah, yes, then they are a deep rich brown colour and shining as though they have been polished and that is the time to gather them by the bucketful.

Pierced, pickled and threaded onto a bootlace, the big, burnished seeds of the horse chestnut (*Aesculus hippocastanum*) were the pride and joy of schoolchildren everywhere, though the game was dying out when Roald Dahl wrote his final book *My Year*. Richmal Crompton's schoolboy hero-cum-rogue William Brown, perpetually 11 years old, is the quintessential conker player.

8 September

billy-wix

An East Anglian word for a tawny owl (see 12 September) or sometimes a barn owl (*Tyto alba*), yet another example of the affectionate practice of giving bird species human first names.

9 September

harvest moon

The European name for September's full moon is typically the harvest moon, though the term barley moon is also widespread.

10 September

auburn

> Sweet Auburn! parent of the blissful hour,
> Thy glades forlorn confess the tyrant's power.
> Here as I take my solitary rounds,
> Amidst thy tangling walks, and ruined grounds,
> And, many a year elapsed, return to view
> Where once the cottage stood, the hawthorn grew

A classic autumnal colour. Auburn, oddly, derives from Latin *albus*, white, taking on the meaning 'red-brown' in the 16th century because 'auburn' and 'brown' sounded similar. The word was chosen by poet Oliver Goldsmith as the name of the village in his 1770 poem 'The Deserted Village'. The poem is a social commentary on rural depopulation as countryfolk move to seek opportunities in the cities and America, but the images the poet captures of nature reclaiming the streets are rather lovely to our modern eye.

11 September

brume

An old poetic word for one of those Keatsian mists (see this month's introduction), from the French. We may wonder why English bothered to borrow it – given the language's own great number of misty and foggy words.

12 September

hoolet

> In September dawns I hardly breathe – I am an image in a ball of glass. The world is suspended there, and I in it. Once, on a night of such clear silence, long past midnight, lying awake outside the tent, my eyes on the plateau where an afterwash of light was lingering, I heard in the stillness a soft, an almost imperceptible thud. It was enough to make me turn my head. There on the tent pole a tawny owl stared down at me. I could just discern his shape against the sky. I stared back. He turned his head about, now one eye upon me, now the other, then melted down into the air so silently that had I not been watching him I could not have known he was gone. To have heard the movement of the midnight owl – that was rare, it was a minor triumph.

Nan Shepherd's encounter with a tawny owl (*Strix aluco*) while camping in the Grampians – recounted in *The Living Mountain* – is typical of her relation to nature – immersive, both physically and spiritually. Shepherd draws attention to the near-silent flight of this nocturnal predator. Hootlet is a Scots word for the tawny owl.

earsh

Who hath not seen thee oft amid thy store?
  Sometimes whoever seeks abroad may find
Thee sitting careless on a granary floor,
  Thy hair soft-lifted by the winnowing wind;
Or on a half-reap'd furrow sound asleep,
  Drows'd with the fume of poppies, while thy hook
    Spares the next swath and all its twined flowers:
And sometimes like a gleaner thou dost keep
  Steady thy laden head across a brook;
  Or by a cyder-press, with patient look,
    Thou watchest the last oozings hours by hours.

Where are the songs of spring? Ay, Where are they?
  Think not of them, thou hast thy music too, –
While barred clouds bloom the soft-dying day,
  And touch the stubble-plains with rosy hue

In his ode 'To Autumn', John Keats imagines the personified autumn resting in the granary or by the cider press, her work done, the crops harvested and the fields gleaned, with only the stubble remaining in the fields to be touched by the rosy hue of the soft-dying day.

In south-west England, a stubble field was once known as an earsh – a word commonly found on old medieval tithe maps.

14 September

cornucopia

The cornucopia – meaning 'horn of plenty' – has been a symbol of autumnal abundance and fruitfulness since ancient times. In Greek mythology, the 'original' horn was created when the infant Zeus accidentally broke off one of the horns of his wet nurse, the goat-nymph Amalthea, and it subsequently had the power to provide unending nourishment. A more prosaic explanation of its origin lies in the horn-shaped baskets that farmers wore on their backs during the harvest.

15 September

bent

> 'When the pigeons go a-benting
> Then the farmers lie lamenting'

In East Anglia, the dry stalks of grass remaining in the pastures after the summer harvest were known as bents. In years that the pigeons had to turn to scavenging the bents in the fields instead of feeding on corn, as the proverb goes, farmers would be lamenting a bad harvest.

16 September

mizzle

It rains in autumn... of course it does – and increasingly so in our changing climate – but we like to think of it as gentle, misty rain, adding to the season's melancholy. English has the perfect word for this, 'mizzle' – the same as 'drizzle' but a less dreary and more poetic way to get a soaking.

17 September

spinney

> There was warmth and ripeness in the air. Autumn was burning across the Vale, the beeches flaring like torches as the heat mist ebbed away from hedges and spinneys and from flocks grazing along the slopes of the faded fields. Yet, unwilling as I was to acknowledge it, I knew now that this landscape was fixed only momentarily.

J L Carr's *A Month in the Country* is his best-known novel, in which an ex-soldier, in the aftermath of World War I, finds some healing when he works to uncover a whitewashed mural in an English parish church. The landscape – on the cusp of summer and autumn – underscores the brevity and fragility of life that is one of the novel's leitmotifs.

A spinney is a word for a copse or small wood used for game cover – from Old French *espinei*, meaning a thorny thicket.

18 September — aplochs

Scots word for the tricky corners of a cornfield or meadow that can't be shorn or mown. Traditionally, they were left as an apotropaic offering to warlocks and other evil spirits, so they did no harm to the land or farmer.

19 September — mellow

Season of mists and mellow fruitfulness,
  Close bosom-friend of the maturing sun;
Conspiring with him how to load and bless
  With fruit the vines that round the thatch-eves run;
To bend with apples the moss'd cottage-trees,
  And fill all fruit with ripeness to the core;
    To swell the gourd, and plump the hazel shells
  With a sweet kernel; to set budding more,
And still more, later flowers for the bees,
Until they think warm days will never cease,
  For Summer has o'er-brimm'd their clammy cells.

This is the opening stanza from the most famous autumn poem of all, John Keats' ode 'To Autumn', written on 19 September 1819. Despite ill-health and financial worries, the poem conveys a rich sense of contentment, even rapture, as the poet engages with the fullness and bounty of the season.

To an extent, Keats has shaped our ideas of what early autumn is – all mists and fruitfulness – when at least the present reality of September is that it is often very rainy, even stormy. The softness of the Keatsian autumn is all bound up in the word 'mellow', whose etymological origins, appropriately here, lie in ancient words for milled flour and ripe juiciness. For another Keats take on autumn, see 21 September.

20 September — rumescent

> Is not this a true autumn day? Just the still melancholy that I love – that makes life and nature harmonise. The birds are consulting about their migrations, the trees are putting on the hectic or the pallid hues of decay, and begin to strew the ground, that one's very footsteps may not disturb the repose of earth and air, while they give us a scent that is a perfect anodyne to the restless spirit. Delicious autumn! My very soul is wedded to it, and if I were a bird I would fly about the earth seeking the successive autumns.

If this quotation from one of her letters is anything to go by, George Eliot (pen name of Mary Ann Evans) loved the earthy, musky smell of freshly fallen autumn leaves – though she did not yet have the word 'rumescent' to describe it. The word is a recent neologism and hasn't yet made its way into any dictionary.

21 September — stubble

> How beautiful the season is now. How fine the air – a temperate sharpness about it. Really, without joking – Dian skies. I never liked stubble-fields so much as now – aye, better than the chilly green of the Spring. Somehow, a stubble plain looks warm, in the same way that some pictures look warm. This struck me so much in my Sunday's walk that I composed upon it.

The sight of harvested fields, the expanse of roughly hewn stalks showing the bare earth beneath – may leave us feeling that winter is not far away. For Keats, though, the richness of the soil emphasized autumn's warm tawny tones, reminding him, he says, of paintings – he was perhaps thinking of works by his contemporary John Constable. The word 'stubble' comes from the Latin *stipula*, stalk or straw.

The composition, inspired by Keats' Sunday walk in countryside near Winchester, is 'To Autumn' (see 19 September).

22 September

sallow

It is a willow when summer is over,
a willow by the river
from which no leaf has fallen nor
bitten by the sun
turned orange or crimson.
The leaves cling and grow paler,
swing and grow paler
over the swirling waters of the river
as if loath to let go,
they are so cool, so drunk with
the swirl of the wind and of the river –
oblivious to winter,
the last to let go and fall
into the water and on the ground.

In 'Willow Poem', William Carlos Williams celebrates the willow (*Salix* spp.) as seeming to continue the summer because its leaves stay longest and greenest. Some broader-leaved willows are known as sallows, from the Latin *salix*, though the roots lie in still older words for 'grey or dusky green' – words that also developed into that other 'sallow', meaning sickly-looking.

23 September

psithurism

A word to reach for, perhaps, when an autumn wind is blowing gently through dry leaves, this one from the Greek *psithurizein* 'to whisper'. Lovely as it is, like many such words, it is a coinage minted by a Victorian fellow with too much knowledge of Classical languages and too much time on his hands. Rustle does the job admirably and onomatopoeically.

24 September

decuman

And then the two
Dropt to the cove, and watched the great sea fall,
Wave after wave, each mightier than the last,
Till last, a ninth one, gathering half the deep
And full of voices, slowly rose and plunged
Roaring, and all the wave was in a flame:
And down the wave and in the flame was borne
A naked babe, and rode to Merlin's feet,
Who stoopt and caught the babe, and cried 'The King!
Here is an heir for Uther!'

In Alfred, Lord Tennyson's 'The Coming of Arthur', the first poem in his cycle *Idylls of the King*, Merlin thus plucks the infant Arthur out of the wild sea at Tintagel, Cornwall. In Irish mythology, the Ninth Wave marked the threshold between our world and the Otherworld, and its inclusion here underlines Arthur's supernatural origins. Perhaps we can count one wave larger still with the decuman, or tenth, wave – from the Latin *decumanus* 'of the tenth', but which can be used for any particularly powerful wave.

25 September

tsukimi

In Japanese Heian period courtly culture, 'moon-viewing' – *tsukimi* – parties were held to celebrate and honour the autumn full moon, accompanied by poetry and music, as well as by food. The parties sometimes took place on boats floating on a lake so that the moon's reflection could be admired in the water. The parties had a strong spiritual, contemplative aspect as well, with the moon honoured as the guardian of the harvest.

Tsukimi are still widely celebrated today: homes are decorated with pampas grass and rice dumplings are served. Many towns and cities hold civic moon viewings in parks and gardens.

26 September — quince

They dined on mince, and slices of quince,
  Which they ate with a runcible spoon;
And hand in hand, on the edge of the sand,
  They danced by the light of the moon,
    The moon,
    The moon,
They danced by the light of the moon.

Edward Lear's famous nonsense poem 'The Owl and the Pussy-Cat' ends with the odd couple celebrating their wedding by feasting on mince and quince and dancing on a beach under the moonlight. The quince (*Cydonia oblonga*) has become an unjustly neglected autumn fruit: half-apple, half-pear, and bullet hard even when ripe, it becomes luscious and deeply fragrant when slowly cooked: a lovely addition to an apple pie or when used to make membrillo, the Spanish quince paste served with cheese. In ancient Greece, the fruit was sacred to Aphrodite, so Lear's choice of fruit here for a wedding breakfast is not just about the 'silly' rhyme.

27 September — kawagiri

So thickly lies the morning mist,
That I can scarcely see
The fish-nets on the river bank,
The River of Uji,
Past daybreak though it be.

Japanese term for an early-autumn mist rising from a river. This poem is by the Heian-period Japanese poet Fujiwara no Sadayori.

28 SEPTEMBER

stook

Summer ends now; now, barbarous in beauty, the stooks arise
Around; up above, what wind-walks! what lovely behaviour
Of silk-sack clouds! has wilder, wilful-wavier
Meal-drift moulded ever and melted across skies?

A stook is a collection of six or eight sheaves – bundles of cut grain-stalks – that lean against one another to keep the grain-heads off the ground, so that they can dry and cure for a few days before being taken for threshing. Gerard Manley Hopkins' poem 'Hurrahing in Harvest' describes a walk on a windy, cloudy day in September. Quite why the stooks are 'barbarous' isn't clear, though perhaps he is thinking of them as like pagan monuments to harvest gods.

gentian

Not every man has gentians in his house
in Soft September, at slow, Sad Michaelmas.

Bavarian gentians, big and dark, only dark
darkening the daytime torchlike with the smoking blueness of Pluto's gloom,
ribbed and torch-like, with their blaze of darkness spread blue
down flattening into points, flattened under the sweep of white day
torch-flower of the blue-smoking darkness, Pluto's dark-blue daze,
black lamps from the halls of Dis, burning dark blue,
giving off darkness, blue darkness, as Demeter's pale lamps give off light,
lead me then, lead me the way.

Reach me a gentian, give me a torch
let me guide myself with the blue, forked torch of this flower
down the darker and darker stairs, where blue is darkened on blueness,
even where Persephone goes, just now, from the frosted September
to the sightless realm where darkness is awake upon the dark
and Persephone herself is but a voice
or a darkness invisible enfolded in the deeper dark
of the arms Plutonic, and pierced with the passion of dense gloom,
among the splendour of torches of darkness, shedding
darkness on the lost bride and her groom.

Michaelmas traditionally marked the end of harvest and thus the slow descent into winter. In his poem 'Bavarian Gentians' (written in September 1929, when he was gravely ill and recuperating in the Bavarian Alps, not long before his death), D H Lawrence celebrates the deep-blue autumn flowering *Gentiana bavarica* as his 'torch-flower' guiding the way into the underworld and to coming death. According to Pliny the Elder, the name of the gentian derived from Gentius, a king of Illyria (the western Balkans), who discovered – supposedly – the medicinal properties of the plant. It may be that Lawrence had this association in mind in his poem.

30 September

rutilant

In the other gardens
  And all up in the vale,
From the autumn bonfires
  See the smoke trail!

Pleasant summer over,
  And all the summer flowers,
The red fire blazes,
  The grey smoke towers.

Sing a song of seasons!
  Something bright in all!
Flowers in the summer,
  Fires in the fall!

Robert Louis Stevenson's simple, graceful children's poem 'Autumn Fires' – full of bonfire smoke and rutilant (fiery-red) tones – leads us into October, the latter half of autumn when the leaves fall quickly and the chill begins to bite.

October

It is autumn in Moominvalley, for how else can spring come back again?

– Tove Jansson, *Finn Family Moomintroll*

Autumn is traditionally the season of wistfulness. In September, summer is still fresh in our minds and the bounty of fruit and nuts lulls us into complacency. By October, though, it seems long, long ago and winter lurks just around the corner of a muddy lane. All of nature seems to be dying in front of our eyes. Storms with friendly-sounding names, but bad tempers, arrive in quick succession.

But October has its consolations: the glorious beauty of the changing leaves – a volcanic eruption of colour before the ashen grey of winter. The 19th-century American writer Henry David Thoreau even called October 'the month of painted leaves'. In Japan, Finland, New England and many other places, people seek out the spectacular autumn colour shows – leaf-peeping (see 28 October) as the Americans say, or 'red-leaf hunting' (see 15 October), in Japan. It's as if by drinking in all that furious colour we can store it in our memories through the winter months...until the spring comes back again.

1 October — nutkin

> One autumn when the nuts were ripe, and the leaves on the hazel bushes were golden and green – Nutkin and Twinkleberry and all the other little squirrels came out of the wood, and down to the edge of the lake.

Beatrix Potter's *The Tale of Squirrel Nutkin* – in which the eponymous hero and his friends, in search of nuts, make a daring raid on an island involving rafts, sacks and other un-squirrelly things – may lack zoological accuracy but it shows us how we should start out on the daunting month of October: with the spirit of adventure. Let the red-tailed Squirrel Nutkin be your month's mascot.

2 October — fall

> O hushed October morning mild,
> Thy leaves have ripened to the fall;
> Tomorrow's wind, if it be wild,
> Should waste them all.

If the English word for the season is lovely but opaque, the American word – beautiful, too – is as clear as... well, falling leaves. The opening stanza of US poet Robert Frost's 'October' captures all the month's precarious beauty.

3 October

ruddy

Oh Rowan tree! Oh, Rowan tree! thou'lt aye be dear to me.

How fair wert thou in simmer time, wi' a' thy clusters white,
How rich and gay thy autumn dress, wi' berries red and bright,
We sat aneath thy spreading shade, the bairnies round thee ran;
They pu'd thy bonnie berries red, and necklaces they strang.
Oh Rowan tree! Oh, Rowan tree! thou'lt aye be dear to me.

On thy fair stem were mony names, which now nae mair I see,
But they're engraven on my heart, forgot they ne'er can be!
My mother! oh! I see her still, she smil'd our sports to see;
Wi' little Jeanie on her lap, wi' Jamie at her knee!
Oh Rowan tree! Oh, Rowan tree! thou'lt aye be dear to me.

Here, Scottish lyricist Lady Nairne, a contemporary of Robert Burns, celebrates the rowan tree's change from white flowers to red berries, and the custom of engraving the names of departed loved ones into the tree bark. The name 'rowan' comes ultimately from a Proto-Indo-European root, **reudh-*, meaning 'ruddy'.

4 October

dunker

The Northern Isles of Scotland – Orkney and Shetland – are near enough treeless so autumn makes itself known in the rainy mists and misty rains that sweep over these bare but beautiful islands. The old language of these places was Norn – a descendant of Old Norse now sadly extinct – and was especially rich (or waterlogged) in misty and rainy words. A dunker was an intense, dense mist that crept through the seams of your clothes.

hydref

My birthday began with the water-
Birds and the birds of the winged trees flying my name
Above the farms and the white horses
And I rose
In rainy autumn
And walked abroad in a shower of all my days.
High tide and the heron dived when I took the road
Over the border
And the gates
Of the town closed as the town awoke.

A springful of larks in a rolling
Cloud and the roadside bushes brimming with whistling
Blackbirds and the sun of October
Summery
On the hill's shoulder,
Here were fond climates and sweet singers suddenly
Come in the morning where I wandered and listened
To the rain wringing
Wind blow cold
In the wood faraway under me.

– Dylan Thomas, 'Poem in October'

The Welsh know how to add wonder to the world. Forget falling leaves and harvests – their word for autumn, *hydref*, is made up of *hydd*, meaning 'stag', and *fref*, meaning 'bellow' (see 31 October) – hence autumn is the 'season of the stag's bellow'. And indeed, autumn is the rutting season when stags call out in the woods, using deep, sonorous cries to attract a mate. It is the sound we might imagine an angry Jabberwock making (see 6 October), in addition to the whiffling and burbling.

6 October

tulgey

And as in uffish thought he stood,
The Jabberwock, with eyes of flame,
Came whiffling through the tulgey wood,
And burbled as it came!

Among the cornucopia of nonsense words in Lewis Carroll's poem 'Jabberwocky' is tulgey, though what better word to describe the creeping dense darkness as we walk through woodland as the nights draw in? The word is perhaps a portmanteau of 'turgid' and 'bulgy', though it has been ingeniously, if improbably, derived from the Anglo-Cornish word for darkness, *tulgu*.

7 October

yaffingale

I once a King and chief
Now am the tree-bark's thief,
Ever 'twixt trunk and leaf
Chasing the prey.

The European green woodpecker (*Picus viridis*) is a striking bird, known variously as a yaffingale, yaffle, rain-bird or weather cock. The first two folk names refer to the bird's laughing call, whilst the latter relate to its supposed ability to induce rain. Its Latin name, *Picus*, relates to the mythical Roman king Picus, referenced in William Morris' tapestry poem 'The Woodpecker', who spurned the love of the witch Circe and was transformed into a woodpecker.

8 October

smirr

A smirr is a fine misty rain – or snow, in this case, in the opening stanza from the Scots poem by David Rorie, 'The Cynic'. It's the perfect evocation of a miserable, windy day with a bite in the air.

> Cauld blew the blast frae East to Wast,
> A blast wi' a smirr o' snaw,
> An' it took the doctor's guid lum hat
> Richt owre the kirk-yaird wa'.

9 October

squash

This is the time of year when, out on a country walk, we might see the gorgeous spectacle of a pumpkin field (see also 30 October) – row upon row of red-golden swollen squash. We might want the generic word 'squash' – used for all sorts of colourful gourds – to evoke the mushy texture of these vegetable-fruits when cooked, but the word is in fact a truncated version of *asquutasquash*, borrowed from the Narragansett people of what is now the US state of Rhode Island. For many Indigenous peoples of the Americas, the fruit was a staple food – along with corn (maize) and beans, one of the 'three sisters'. We can see why the first English colonists, on being introduced to the fruit, soon shortened its name, but to honour its Indigenous origins perhaps we should learn it afresh. Try it: *ask-ul-tuh-skwosh*.

10 October

duff

Duff is the layer of decaying matter on a woodland or forest floor, above the mineral soil and below the fresh leaf litter. It plays a vital role in the sylvian ecosystem, retaining moisture like a sponge and providing a home to all sorts of organisms including fungi. It's also the stuff most likely to cause you to slip over during a rainy woodland walk.

11 October

acorn

The acorn, with its deep-brown nut and 'knitted' cup (cupule), is one of the familiar sights on an autumn woodland floor. It's nutritious fodder for all sorts of animals and provides us humans with a well-worn metaphoric cliché, as in these lines by Victorian poet Francis William Bourdillon:

> An acorn swung
> On an oak-tree bough;
> So long it had hung,
> It would fain fall now
> To the kindly earth,
> That its germ within
> Might burst into birth,
> And its life begin.

Compare the much pithier proverb: 'Mighty oaks from little acorns grow'.

12 October — hunter's moon

The Hunter's Moon rides low,
  Her course is nearly sped.
Where is the panting roe?
  Where hath the wild deer fled?
Hunter and hunted now
    Lie in oblivion deep:
    Dead or asleep.

Autumn is the hunting season, so October's full moon – when huntsmen could continue their pursuit of game through the night – was called the hunter's moon. The closing stanza of 'Hunter's Moon' by the 19th-century German-born English writer Mathilde Blind imagines the close of a just such a night – thrilling for some, devastating for others.

13 October — orchard

Midst bitten mead and acre shorn,
The world without is waste and worn,

But here within our orchard-close,
The guerdon of its labour shows.

O valiant Earth, O happy year
That mocks the threat of winter near,

And hangs aloft from tree to tree
The banners of the Spring to be.

The harvest may been brought in from the meadow (mead), and the farmers' acres shorn, but the orchard is still bountiful at this time of year, although winter is looming, as this poem by William Morris demonstrates. The word orchard takes its root from **wurt-* (plant) **gard* (enclosure).

14 October — twilight

Over it the Star of Evening
Melts and trembles through the purple,
Hangs suspended in the twilight.
No; it is a bead of wampum
On the robes of the Great Spirit
As he passes through the twilight,
Walks in silence through the heavens.

Venus, the evening star, figures prominently in Henry Wadsworth Longfellow's *The Song of Hiawatha*, representing the divine and mystical. As the days shorten and the twilight hour comes earlier, October is the perfect time to gaze to the heavens.

15 October — *momijigari*

irozuku ya	changed to red they
tōfu ni ochite	fall gently on my tofu
usu momiji	light autumn leaves

Just as the Japanese hold blossom-viewing parties in spring (see 8 May), they take part in leaf-viewing parties in autumn. This tradition is called *momijigari* – red-leaf hunting – and dates back to the Heian period, when the wealthy and posh pinicked and wrote poetry under the changing trees. Deep-red maple leaves were a particular favourite.

The turning leaves had a spiritual meaning – expressing the transience of life – and inspired haiku like the one above by the 17th-century master Matsuo Bashō. The poet is dining al fresco under a maple tree and a leaf falls into a dish of tofu. Annoying for the picnickers, you might think, but for Bashō it creates a striking contrast of red on white and a reason for a typically Zen meditation on death in life.

The Finnish have a similar tradition, as we shall see on 18 October.

16 October

plothering

There must surely be a law governing the relationship between the number of weather words in a language and the climate its speakers enjoy or, more likely, endure. The peoples of the Arctic are famous for their rich vocabulary of snow ('fifty words' and all that) and other teeth-chattering phenomena, discerning kinds and varieties that would be invisible to someone, say, from sunny Italy.

Inevitably, then, across the well-sodden islands of Britain and Ireland, the linguistic weather treasuries are well stocked with pluvious words, covering not just intensity but length. One such word in English is plothering, a Midlands and North-East dialect word for...wait for it... the heavy rain that falls in big, splashy drops when no wind is blowing.

Keep an eye open for the size of the raindrops next time it pours (that'll probably be this afternoon!).

17 October

wanwood

Márgarét, áre you grieving
Over Goldengrove unleaving?
Leáves, like the things of man, you
With your fresh thoughts care for, can you?
Ah! ás the heart grows older
It will come to such sights colder
By and by, nor spare a sigh
Though worlds of wanwood leafmeal lie;
And yet you will weep and know why.

The late Victorian poet Gerard Manley Hopkins was both a nature and word lover (the two so often go hand in hand) and peppered his verse with coinages as he sought to capture the Earth's wonders – wonders he considered to be an expression of God's love. In these alliteration-rich lines from his poem 'Spring and Fall', the word 'wanwood' refers to a dying woodland ('wan' means pale or sickly), while leafmeal – a play on piecemeal – means 'leaf by leaf'.

18 OCTOBER

ruska

The Finnish term for the colouring autumn leaves, of which the Finnish are very fond. Thank heavens, for much of the country is covered in deciduous trees – birch, larch, aspen and maple.

19 OCTOBER

dungel

A Norn word for the mist that appears on top of a hill.

20 OCTOBER

marcescent

A scientific word used to describe withering leaves that are still attached to the tree, and so sometimes used metaphorically as an image of human resilience.

21 OCTOBER

pomona

I am the ancient Apple-Queen,
As once I was so am I now.
For evermore a hope unseen,
Betwixt the blossom and the bough.

Ah, where's the river's hidden Gold!
And where the windy grave of Troy?
Yet come I as I came of old,
From out the heart of Summer's joy.

The 21st October is apple day in the UK – an annual celebration of apples and orchards. The Apple-Queen referenced here by William Morris is Pomona – the Roman goddess of fruit trees, gardens, abundance and plenty, who has now become associated with cider making and apple orchards. Her name comes from the Latin for fruit, *pomum*.

22 OCTOBER

bange

Fog everywhere. Fog up the river, where it flows among green aits and meadows; fog down the river, where it rolls defiled among the tiers of shipping and the waterside pollutions of a great (and dirty) city. Fog on the Essex marshes, fog on the Kentish heights. Fog creeping into the cabooses of collier-brigs; fog lying out on the yards and hovering in the rigging of great ships; fog drooping on the gunwales of barges and small boats.

In East Anglia, known for its vast fenlands and dank marshlands, heavy mists can roll in from the North Sea and linger for days, making this lonesome landscape yet eerier. These are known as banges. Charles Dickens evoked these rolling fogs in the haunting opening to *Bleak House*.

23 OCTOBER — stodge

In autumn, we are liable to fill up on stodgy comfort food – cottage pie, followed by blackberry-and-apple crumble, anyone? – but in English dialect it is sometimes used to describe the heavy, puddingy mud along a track or path that's hard to walk through. Especially if you've eaten too much of the aforementioned fare.

24 OCTOBER — wuthering

> The storm came rattling over the Heights in full fury. There was a violent wind, as well as thunder, and either one or the other split a tree off at the corner of the building; a huge bough fell across the roof, and knocked down a portion of the east chimney-stack, sending a clatter of stones and soot into the kitchen fire.

The wild wuthering winds of autumn are almost a character in themselves in Emily Brontë's gothic novel, and give their evocative name to both the setting and the book. Wuthering comes from the Old Norse **hviðra* meaning a squall of wind, and the theme runs through the book, echoing the stormy passions of *Wuthering Heights'* Cathy and Heathcliff.

25 OCTOBER gloaming

Some words seem only to be used by poets at their most poetical, and gloaming, meaning (evening) twilight, is one of these. It's a word with pedigree – the Old English *glōmung* – and simultaneously manages to evoke both glowing light and gloom. Here it is used by the fine but now near-forgotten Irish writer Katharine Tynan in the poem 'The Children of Lir', which has an autumnal air of loss and restlessness:

> On the chilly lakelet, in that pleasant gloaming,
> See the sad swans sailing: they shall have no rest:
> Never a voice to greet them save the bittern's booming
> Where the ghostly sallows sway against the West.

26 OCTOBER driech

A well-known Scottish word to describe dreary, grey weather – used by Scottish people as a matter of course, and by English people to show their cosmopolitanism.

skein

'Oh tell me what was on yer road, ye roarin' norlan' Wind,
As ye cam' blawin' frae the land that's niver frae my mind?
My feet they traivel England, but I'm deein' for the north.'
'My man, I heard the siller tides rin up the Firth o Forth.'

'Aye, Wind, I ken them weel eneuch, and fine they fa' and rise,
And fain I'd feel the creepin' mist on yonder shore that lies,
But tell me, ere ye passed them by, what saw ye on the way?'
'My man, I rocked the rovin' gulls that sail abune the Tay.'

'But saw ye naething, leein' Wind, afore ye cam' to Fife?
There's muckle lyin' 'yont the Tay that's mair to me nor life.'
'My man, I swept the Angus braes ye hae'na trod for years.'
'O Wind, forgi'e a hameless loon that canna see for tears!'

'And far abune the Angus straths I saw the wild geese flee,
A lang, lang skein o' beatin' wings, wi' their heids towards the sea,
And aye their cryin' voices trailed ahint them on the air –'
'O Wind, hae maircy, haud yer whisht, for I daurna listen mair!'

In her poem 'The Wild Geese', the aristocratic Scots poet Violet Jacob conjures the blustery shores of her homeland, and in the final stanza the arrowhead flight of honking geese – one of the wonders of the autumn sky. A skein is ordinarily a length of yarn that has been wound and then loosley twisted around itself, but has long also been applied to the V-shaped formation of flying geese, perhaps because it looks as though said yarn is unravelling across the sky.

28 October

leaf peeping

Touristic trips to view the glorious colours of fall leaves in New England and elsewhere first became popular in the 19th century, and by the 1930s foliage festivals were popping up everywhere (the cynic might say to extend the tourist season). The word 'leaf-peaker' to describe these tree-chasers turned up in the 1960s, but 'leaf-peeper' soon won the day (thankfully, 'leaf-voyeur' didn't make the cut).

29 October

ramballiach

Next time the weather is wild and windy, be sure to use the Scots word 'ramballiach', meaning tempestuous. No one is sure of its origin, but it conjures up images of rampant, rumbustious winds and justifies taking the consolation of a wee dram or two by the fire.

30 October

pumpkin

> Oh, fruit loved of boyhood! the old days recalling,
> When wood-grapes were purpling and brown nuts were falling!
> When wild, ugly faces we carved in its skin,
> Glaring out through the dark with a candle within!

These lines by the charmingly named American poet John Greenleaf Whittier remind us it's time to carve out those jack o'lanterns, ready to scare off the ghosts, ghouls and witches that are bound to come calling at Halloween.

bellow

'Bellow' is an ancient onomatopoeic word used to describe the roar of an animal (see 5 October), but is easily used for other loud sounds, here loud, jump-out-of-your-skin thunder:

> The wind blew as twad blawn its last;
> The rattling show'rs rose on the blast;
> The speedy gleams the darkness swallow'd;
> Loud, deep, and lang the thunder bellow'd:
> That night, a child might understand,
> The Deil had business on his hand.

Robert Burns' *Tam O'Shanter* – about a reckless farmer, Tam, riding home drunk after market-day in Ayr – is the perfect Halloween poem, even if the exact time of year is left unspecified. It's dark, stormy and pouring with rain... and – the biggest clue – witches are dancing with the Devil ('Deil') in a lonesome kirk.

Like it or not, October ends in darkness and disorder.

November

No sun – no moon!
No morn – no noon –
No dawn – no dusk – no proper time of day.

No warmth, no cheerfulness, no healthful ease,
No comfortable feel in any member –
No shade, no shine, no butterflies, no bees,
No fruits, no flowers, no leaves, no birds! –
November!

– Thomas Hood, 'November'

We are at the fag-end of autumn – when even the season of fruitfulness has exhausted itself. It is another month of transition. The leaves have now almost all fallen and autumn colour is muted. The nights draw in fast, and wintry weather begins to take hold. In the morning, sharp frosts glisten on the hedgerows, and those pretty, wispy mists turn to impenetrable fogs. Foxes yowl and rooks craw.

Thomas Hood's poem 'November' – essentially a list of negatives – humorously draws attention to its absences – aren't we all just marking time until the festivities of December? – but a good, bracing walk will show us that even this month has its grace notes.

myst-hakel

Myst-hakel means 'mist-cloak' in Middle English and makes its appearance in the fine medieval poem *Sir Gawain and the Green Knight*, when the hero – King Arthur's nephew – sets out on his quest to meet the Green Knight and an almost certain death by beheading. The landscape he passes through is suitably driech (see 26 October).

The lines in which myst-hakel appears are worth attempting out loud (note: the letter þ – thorn – is equivalent to a 'th'):

> Mist muged on þe mor, malt on þe mountez,
> Vch hille hade a hatte, a myst-hakel huge.

In his translation, the Poet Laureate Simon Armitage renders myst-hakel as 'hat of mizzle':

> so the moors and the mountains were muzzy with mist
> and every hill wore a hat of mizzle on its head.

beaver moon

> November, the Beaver Moon; for in this month the beavers begin to take shelter in their houses, having laid up a sufficient store of provisions for the winter season.

– Jonathan Carver, *Travels Through the Interior Parts of North-America, in the Years 1766, 1767, and 1768*

November's full moon is the beaver moon or the frost moon. Beavers (*Castor fiber*) had disappeared from Britain by the 16th century (and in England much earlier), hunted to extinction not only for their fur and meat but the vanilla-scented secretion known as castoreum, used in perfume making. Beavers were never native to Ireland.

In the last few years, however, populations have been re-established across the country as part of managed reintroduction programmes, aimed in part to sustain fragile wetlands and to help with flood management. Soon, perhaps, we will once again be able to spy beavers busying themselves on waterways on moon-bright November nights.

tawny

> Anne's object was, not to be in the way of anybody; and where the narrow paths across the fields made many separations necessary, to keep with her brother and sister. Her pleasure in the walk must arise from the exercise and the day, from the view of the last smiles of the year upon the tawny leaves, and withered hedges, and from repeating to herself some few of the thousand poetical descriptions extant of autumn, that season of peculiar and inexhaustible influence on the mind of taste and tenderness, that season which had drawn from every poet, worthy of being read, some attempt at description, or some lines of feeling.

Jane Austen's *Persuasion*, from which this quotation comes, is the novelist's most autumnal book – being about the rekindling of love in 'later' life (even if the heroine, Anne Elliot, is just 28). It also includes a famous late-autumn scene Upper Cross, Somerset, in which the poetry-loving Anne – almost resigned to her unmarried state – takes part in, for her, a melancholy walk with family members and her estranged former fiancé, Captain Wentworth.

The word 'tawny', used to describe the leaves derives from the yellowy-brown colour of tanned leather, and more remotely from Celtic words for oak tree, as in the Breton *tann*.

heron

In the cloud-grey mornings
I heard the herons flying;
And when I came into my garden,
My silken outer-garment
Trailed over withered leaves.
A dried leaf crumbles at a touch,
But I have seen many Autumns
With herons blowing like smoke
Across the sky.

In November herons become more visible as they feed, statue-like, in wetlands or estuaries, or as they track across the sky southward in search of new hunting grounds. The herons 'blowing like smoke' in the American poet Amy Lowell's 'Hoarfrost' are likely the great blue (*Ardea herodias*), while in Britain and Ireland it is the grey heron (*Ardea cinerea*) that command the rivers and skies.

5 November

frost

The door was shut, as doors should be,
Before you went to bed last night;
Yet Jack Frost has got in, you see,
And left your window silver white.

He must have waited till you slept;
And not a single word he spoke,
But pencilled o'er the panes and crept
Away again before you woke.

And now you cannot see the hills
Nor fields that stretch beyond the lane;
But there are fairer things than these
His fingers traced on every pane.

The figure of Jack Frost is perhaps a domesticated memory of the rime giants (see 18 November) of Norse mythology, malevolent spirits of the winter cold. He was once popular as a character in children's rhymes – as in this example from Scottish poet Thomas Nicoll Hepburn (writing under the pseudonym Gabriel Setoun) – though now may be relegated to tinfoil-clad staple of the school pageant.

6 November

Blōtmōnaþ

> Blot-monath is the month of sacrifices, for it was in this month that the cattle which were to be slaughtered were dedicated to the gods.

So St Bede tells us in his *The Reckoning of Time*. In Old English *blót* meant 'to sacrifice' or 'to worship' and refered to rituals, often led by a community's leaders, in which animals were slaughtered to ensure the land's fertility. Such sacrifices were frowned upon by Christians, so it's no wonder that the Old English name was replaced with the much duller Latin one – the ninth (*novem*) month in the Roman calendar.

cyclamen

Slow toads, and cyclamen leaves
Stickily glistening with eternal shadow
Keeping to earth.
Cyclamen leaves
Toad-filmy, earth-iridescent
Beautiful
Frost-filigreed
Spumed with mud
Snail-nacreous
Low down [...]

And up the pallid, sea-blenched Mediterranean stone-slopes
Rose cyclamen, ecstatic fore-runner!
Cyclamens, ruddy-muzzled cyclamens
In little bunches like bunches of wild hares
Muzzles together, ears-aprick
Whispering witchcraft
Like women at a well, the dawn-fountain.

Greece, and the world's morning
Where all the Parthenon marbles still fostered the roots of
the cyclamen.
Violets
Pagan, rosy-muzzled violets
Autumnal
Dawn-pink,
Dawn-pale
Among squat toad-leaves sprinkling the unborn
Erechtheion marbles.

Hardy cyclamen are one of the great pleasures of November: when the rest of nature is bent on retreat and drabness, the autumn cyclamen – a non-native escapee in British woodlands and hedgerows, present since the 17th century – provides unmissable pops of vibrant colour. In his poem 'Sicilian Cyclamens', D H Lawrence evokes the cyclamen in its native ground (perhaps the autumn-flowering *Cyclamen hederifolium* or spring *Cyclamen repandum*), the Mediterranean, written during his stay in Sicily from 1919 to 1922, the flowers symbolizing the birth of ancient Greek cultures, out of the muddy, frosty earth.

8 November fret

An icy mist that comes in from the North Sea. The word itself has an eerie, 'threatening' sound and may be related to the German word *fressen*, to eat, used for animals.

9 November hoarfrost

Hoarfrost is the feathery white ice crystals that form on cold, still nights when moist, dewy air meets already-freezing vegetation such as leaves and grass, as well as other objects. We may puzzle over its scientific definition, but its effect on our gardens and hedgerows is dazzling, as if overnight nature has been redrawn with a silver graphite pencil.

The Old English word *hoar* meant grey-white, like the salt-and-pepper of a beard – still used in the word 'hoary'.

10 November

zawn

In Cornwall, the deep inlets of the cliffs, cut by erosion and lashed by winter storms are known as zawns – from the Cornish word for chasm and related to the Welsh word for mouth. Cornish poet and priest Robert Stephen Hawker depicted the storm-lashed zawns as bulwarks in the war between the sea and the land in his poem 'The Storm'.

War! 'mid the ocean and the land!
The battle-field Morwenna's strand,
Where rock and ridge the bulwark keep,
The giant warders of the deep!

They come! and shall they not prevail,
The seething surge, the gathering gale?
They fling their wild flag to the breeze,
The banner of a thousand seas!

They come, they mount, they charge in vain,
Thus far, incalculable main!
No more! thine hosts have not o'erthrown
The lichen on the barrier stone!

opium

In Flanders fields, the poppies blow
  Between the crosses, row on row,
 That mark our place; and in the sky
 The larks, still bravely singing, fly
Scarce heard amid the guns below.

We are the Dead. Short days ago
We lived, felt dawn, saw sunset glow,
 Loved and were loved, and now we lie,
    In Flanders fields.
Take up our quarrel with the foe:

To you from failing hands we throw
 The torch; be yours to hold it high.
 If ye break faith with us who die
We shall not sleep, though poppies grow
    In Flanders fields.

Red poppies are, or once were, the flower of summer meadows, but they have also been the flowers of remembrance worn on Armistice Day since 1921. The inspiration for the tradition was the war poem 'In Flanders Fields', written by the Canadian physician Lieutenant-Colonel John McCrae who served during the Second Battle of Ypres.

Paradoxically, in Greek mythology the poppy (*mekon*) was associated not only with death but also forgetting, conjured from the ground by Demeter to help her sleep and forget, for a while, her missing daughter, Persephone. As opium, poppy seeds were used to make the drug of forgetting in Victorian culture and beyond.

12 November — Pleiades

The Moon has left the sky,
Lost is the Pleiads' light;
  It is midnight,
  And time slips by,
But on my couch alone I lie.

This fragment of ancient Greek lyric poetry – composed to be sung to the lyre – is attributed to Sappho and often called the 'Midnight' song. In it the poet seems to allude to the setting of the Pleiades – the stars known as the Seven Sisters – associated in ancient Greece and Rome with the coming of winter, although scholars have argued (of course) at which time of the year the poem is set. The moonless, dark and lonely night does have a Novembery feel, however.

13 November — heavengravel

The weather may be getting cold enough now to give us winter's first taste of hail, or heavengravel as it is poetically named by Gerard Manley Hopkins in 'The Loss Of The Eurydice' his poem commemorating one of Britain's worst peacetime naval disasters.

14 November — chiropteran

Chiropteran is the scientific word you need when describing anything related to bats, from the name of their order, the *Chiroptera* (itself from two ancient Greek words, *kheir* (hand) and *pteron* (wing). By November bats have entered winter hibernation and are hanging, in a deep, deep sleep, in secluded, sheltered spaces such as ruined buildings, caves and tree hollows. If you are fond of a long winter snooze, you might, if you fancy, label it 'chiropteran', too. Do not, on any account, disturb!

15 November — covey

> Here they lie mottled to the ground unseen,
> This covey linked together from the nest.

In autumn and winter grey partridges (*Perdix perdix*) will gather in groups called coveys. Poet Laureate John Masefield's poem 'Partridges' evokes an autumn hunting scene, the covey taken unaware by the guns, with the 'lucky' birds shot clean, the wounded sought out by dogs and the survivors regrouping in darkness.

16 November — rowky

A Cumbrian dialect word meaning a frosty fog. Now imagine yourself out in one and you can feel the cold seeping through your boots and socks.

flavescent

That time of year thou mayst in me behold
When yellow leaves, or none, or few, do hang
Upon those boughs which shake against the cold,
Bare ruin'd choirs, where late the sweet birds sang.

In me thou see'st the twilight of such day
As after sunset fadeth in the west,
Which by and by black night doth take away,
Death's second self, that seals up all in rest.

In me thou see'st the glowing of such fire
That on the ashes of his youth doth lie,
As the death-bed whereon it must expire,
Consum'd with that which it was nourish'd by.

This thou perceiv'st, which makes thy love more strong,
To love that well which thou must leave ere long.

Shakespeare's Sonnet 73 is perhaps the most autumnal in tone, celebrating love that stays the course of time, even into old age (though the poet was only likely in his thirties when he wrote it). The yellow leaves near its beginning may make us think of the word 'flavescent' – turning golden-yellow – from the ancient Greek *flavios* (golden yellow). The word gave its name to the Imperial Roman dynasty the Flavians, beginning with Vespasian (Titus Flavius Vespasianus), one of the better, more effective emperors.

18 November

rime

For scientists ice takes many forms, and one of these is rime, which is rather like, but not quite the same as, hoarfrost (see 9 November), formed in windy, foggy conditions giving it a spiky, punky look (if punks wore white). Rime itself comes in three kinds: hard, soft and clear.

In Norse mythology, the rime (Old English *hrīm*) giants, hrimthursar, were the fiercesome giants of winter, the first and foremost being Ymir born from the icy rivers of Ginnungagap, the primordial void. The Norse and all Germanic peoples took winter very seriously – it was, after all, a matter of life and death.

19 November

rook

There, where the rusty iron lies,
The rooks are cawing all the day.
Perhaps no man, until he dies,
Will understand them, what they say.

The evening makes the sky like clay.
The slow wind waits for night to rise.
The world is half content. But they

Still trouble all the trees with cries,
That know, and cannot put away,
The yearning to the soul that flies
From day to night, from night to day.

Rooks become more evident in November as they gather in large clamorous flocks, in landscapes that otherwise have fallen silent. Their ominous presence is highlighted here in the poem 'Rooks' by the Scottish World War I war poet Charles Hamilton Sorley, killed at the Battle of Loos aged just 20.

20 NOVEMBER — persimmon

Kaki kueba	*I bite a persimmon*
kane ga naru	*and the bell rings out at*
nari Horyuji	*Horyuji temple*

The persimmon (*Diospyros* spp.) is the last fruit of the year, still hanging on the tree after all the leaves have fallen and as such a classic image, in haiku poetry, of both transience and resilience, as in this famous example by Masaoka Shiki.

The lovely English word 'persimmon' was early borrowed from the Algonquian word for the native American persimmon or date-plum (*Diospyros virginiana*) – *pessemmins*, meaning 'dried fruit'.

21 NOVEMBER — vixen

Among the taller wood with ivy hung,
The old fox plays and dances round her young.
She snuffs and barks if any passes by
And swings her tail and turns prepared to fly.
The horseman hurries by, she bolts to see,
And turns agen, from danger never free.
If any stands she runs among the poles
And barks and snaps and drive them in the holes.
The shepherd sees them and the boy goes by
And gets a stick and progs the hole to try.
They get all still and lie in safety sure,
And out again when everything's secure,
And start and snap at blackbirds bouncing by
To fight and catch the great white butterfly.

One of the more unnerving sounds of November, especially in the city, is the ghoulish yowl of male foxes as they search for mates. The word 'vixen' is derived from *fyxe*, the Old English word for a female fox. 'The Vixen' by John Clare evokes the spirit of this wild creature.

22 November

wolflight

> It was dusk – winter dusk. Snow lay white and shining over the pleated hills, and icicles hung from the forest trees. Snow lay piled on the dark road across Willoughby Wood, but from dawn men had been clearing it with brooms and shovels. There were hundreds of them at work, wrapped in sacking because of the bitter cold, and keeping together in groups for fear of the wolves, grown savage and reckless from hunger.

So begins Joan Aitken's classic children's novel *The Wolves of Willoughby Chase*. Set in an alternative 19th century England, packs of wolves menace the frozen countryside, and much of the book's action takes place in the hours of twilight. In Greece dusk is known as *lykófos* – wolflight, whilst the evocative French term is *l'heure entre chien et loup* – the hour between the dog and the wolf – the time when the light is fading and you can no longer tell dog from wolf or friend from foe.

23 November

koharubiyori

The Japanese name for an unseasonal spell of warm weather in November, meaning 'small spring weather'. Enjoy it while you can!

24 November

skump

A Norn word for a bank of fog or grey, gloomy weather – not unknown in the Shetlands and Orkneys where this Norwegian language was once spoken

25 NOVEMBER gluggaveður

An Icelandic word meaning 'window weather', that is, weather that looks much nicer to look at than to be out in – for example a bright November's day that tempts you outside only for you to discover a cold wind is somehow blowing through every seam of your parka.

26 NOVEMBER founther

Freezing in Ulster Scots, as in 'I'm founthered wi tha caul' or 'That day wud founther ye'. It may be related via Old Scots to the French *enfondre* 'to be chilled', although founder also means 'to collapse' in standard English.

27 NOVEMBER abscission

> There was no possibility of taking a walk that day. We had been wandering, indeed, in the leafless shrubbery an hour in the morning; but since dinner (Mrs Reed, when there was no company, dined early) the cold winter wind had brought with it clouds so sombre, and a rain so penetrating, that further out-door exercise was now out of the question.

Another famous November opening in a novel, this one Charlotte Brontë's *Jane Eyre*. The heroine turns out to be a great walker, like all the Brontë sisters, so the ten-year-old Jane's inability to walk as a child suggests the repressive, claustrophobic atmosphere that rules at Gateshead Hall, her loveless early-childhood home.

Abscission is the scientific word for the shedding of leaves and flowers. If we went in for metaphors, we might of think of the young Jane Eyre being abscised from her adopted family home and sent to the wintry prison of Lowood School.

28 November

rustling

In slack wind of November
 The fog forms and shifts;
All the world comes out again
 When the fog lifts.
Loosened from their sapless twigs
 Leaves drop with every gust;
Drifting, rustling, out of sight
 In the damp or dust.

– Christina Rossetti, 'A Year's Windfalls'

As the last of the autumn leaves drop from the trees and the winds send them onomatopoeically rustling, nature starts to put herself into a winter hibernation.

29 November

cranruch

The snow drifted half a yard upon the ground, the trees all white with cranruch like the sugar on a cake.

The Scots for hoarfrost, as recorded here in a story or sketch by the writer Robert Bontine Cunninghame Graham. You might think it's early for snow, but in the Highlands the first snowfalls come as early as September. Brr!

shiver

> There was crisp, dry snow under his feet and more snow lying on the branches of the trees. Overhead there was a pale blue sky, the sort of sky one sees on a fine winter day in the morning. Straight ahead of him he saw between the tree trunks the sun, just rising, very red and clear. Everything was perfectly still, as if he were the only living creature in that country. There was not even a robin or a squirrel among the trees, and the wood stretched as far as he could see in every direction. He shivered.

We may as well face it now, on the very cusp of December as we are: snow. Here, in *The Lion, the Witch and the Wardrobe*, C S Lewis describes Edmund's first sight of the winter-bound Narnia, just before his encounter with the sleigh-riding White Witch, Jadis.

We may well share Edmund's apprehensive shiver as we contemplate the coming winter cold. The modern English 'shiver' may derive from the Old English *ceafl*, jaw, suggesting the chattering of teeth.

December

Fuyugare ya
yo wa isshoku ni
kaze no oto

Withering winter
The world is one-coloured
And the sound of wind.

– Matsuo Bashō

The Japanese word *kogarashi* literally means 'tree withering' and refers to the first really cold wind that ushers in the change from autumn to winter. The last clinging leaves finally fall and the temperature takes a nosedive: all of nature seems to shudder at the thought of the coming winter.

Isn't this the time of retreat, whether into hibernation or the comfort of our homes? Animals need their winter sleep to survive, but from time to time we humans should get out and about – well wrapped-up, of course – to appreciate the season's sights, smells and sounds, its desolation, its beauty. Yes, and stop for a moment and listen to the silence that is not quite silence, and feel the solitude that is not quite solitude.

One again, the Japanese have a word for this wintry bleakness or solitude, *fuyugare*, here recorded in Matsuo Bashō's haiku. Does the winter wind break or make our sense of isolation?

1 DECEMBER

hiernal

'Winter is coming!'

Another of those words invented just to show off a knowledge of Latin, hiernal means wintry, from the Latin *hiems* – though the latter could also signify 'storm'. The phrase 'Winter is coming' is the motto of the ambitious House Stark, rulers of the snowy north of Westeros, in the series of high-fantasy books *A Song of Ice and Fire*, by George R R Martin. For those interested, the motto in Latin would be: *Hiems subest!*

2 DECEMBER

apricity

The concept – the warmth of the sun felt on a winter's day – is wonderful, but the word – from the Latin *apricus*, sun-warmed, is perhaps too rarefied to bother with. It is first recorded in 1623, in Henry Cockeram's *The English Dictionary; or, An Interpreter of Hard English Words*.

3 DECEMBER

bobantilter

In Scots, an icicle and, by extension, any dangling, glittering ornament like earrings.

4 DECEMBER

hibernaculum

Sylvia Plath may well be the only poet to evoke this particular word borrowed from zoology. In this opening stanza from 'Electra on Azalea Path' the imagines retreating from life's griefs into a place of safety through the cold winter months. It comes from the Latin for 'winter residence'. Who hasn't, come these first cold days, thought of snuggling up under the duvet for a few months and seeing the winter blues away?

5 December — brumal

> The robin returns from the land of fire, and therefore he feels the cold of winter far more than his brother birds. He shivers in the brumal blast; hungry, he chirps before your door.

Yet another word for wintry, as if we needed it. This one come from the Latin word for winter, *bruma*. This quotation is taken from *Ancient Legends, Mystic Charms and Superstitions of Ireland*, by Jane Francesca Agnes Wilde, Lady Wilde, the mother of Oscar Wilde.

6 December — brumation

The sluggish, sleepy winter state entered into by reptiles and amphibians such as tortoises (as well as many humans). It's not quite hibernation as the tortoise (for example) will wake up occasionally to drink water.

7 December — heezen

> I freeze, I freeze, and nothing dwells
> In me but snow and icicles.
> For pity's sake, give your advice,
> To melt this snow and thaw this ice.
> I'll drink down flames; but if so be
> Nothing but love can supple me,
> I'll rather keep this frost and snow
> Than to be thaw'd or heated so.

Heezen is a Scots word meaning to shiver with cold, like Robert Herrick does in this wintry love poem 'The Frozen Heart'. The salve for the poet's complaint? Cuddle up closer under the winter blankets.

8 December — nysnö

The Nordic languages are particularly rich in wintry words: it as if the landscape only truly becomes alive in the winter months. This Swedish word means 'new snow' and refers to the first settled snowfall that transforms the autumn world of russet browns and greyish skies to the winter wonderworld of snow-blanketed fields and airy blue skies.

9 December — aquerne

You might think this was an alternative spelling of 'acorn' – see 11 October – but it is in fact the Middle English word for squirrel, derived from Old English *āc-weorn*, meaning 'oak eater'. Squirrels, via French, got the better of *aquernes* soon after. These creatures bury acorns in the autumn and, as they don't hibernate, eat them through the long winter months.

10 December — graupel

> Occasional showers of graupel, sleet, and snow have been recorded.

So went a weather report in 1889, the first recorded use of the word in English. Graupel is a very specific kind of precipitation where water droplets accumulate on falling snowflakes, to create round pellets of softish hail. The word comes from the German verb *graupeln*, to sleet or hail, though it is in fact neither of these things. There's a good debate to be had next time some cold, white stuff falls from the sky.

11 December

sleet

Falling snow that's partly melted or rain that's partly frozen or snow that melts then refreezes? It's much of a muchness by the time it reaches us – it's wet and icy at the same time – and sleet describes it perfectly. The word may come from Old Norse *slydda*, which survives in the wonderful Danish word *slud*, meaning a mix of snow and rain.

12 December

mistletoe

Dimmest and brightest month am I;
My short days end, my lengthening days begin;
What matters more or less sun in the sky,
When all is sun within?
Ivy and privet dark as night,
I weave with hips and haws a cheerful show,
And holly for a beauty and delight,
And milky mistletoe.

So sings the personification of December in Christina Rosetti's 'The Months: A Pageant'. The custom of weaving midwinter wreaths of evergreen plants dates back to the Roman feast of Saturnalia (see 17 December), via the Germanic festival of Yule (21 December). The parasitic plant of mistletoe has long been thought to ward off bad sprits. It has an unfortunate etymology though: as the seeds are spread via the excrement of the mistle thrushes (*Turdus viscivorus*) who eat the berries, the old word 'mistaltan' simply means dung twig.

13 December

ruddock

No bird or even animal is more closely associated to the winter period and Christmas than the robin (*Erithacus rubecula*). Its old name was the ruddock, meaning 'little red one' because of its striking deep-red chest.

The bird got its pet name, Robin ('little Robert') Redbreast, in the 15th century when there was a vogue for giving birds pet human names (including Jenny Wren and Tom Tit), and this, shortened to just robin, entirely supplanted the older name.

Robins began to appear on Christmas cards in the late 19th century, no doubt in part for their festive glow, but also for the red-jacketed British postmen who delivered the cards and were known as 'robins'. The livery colour of the Royal Mail – including those lovely pillar boxes – remains red to this day.

One week or so to the last posting date!

14 December

Niflheim

The next time you feel as though winter has imprisoned you in a world of mist and ice, and the winter chill seems to be gnawing your bones, you might want to reach for the word or name Niflheim. This was one of the primordial realms of Norse mythology, meaning 'mist-world', the other being Muspelheim, fire-world. The related *nifol* was a word in Old English meaning dark and gloomy, but sadly hasn't survived in that sense – though, if I were to coin one such, it would be 'nifling' – as in 'It sure is nifling today', miserably cold.

15 December — issinnirit

Issinnirit are the broken bits of ice that wash up on a beach. This Inuit word shows the importance of linguistic geography – words that reflect the environment of a people.

16 December — skiff

In Scots and elsewhere, a smattering or flurry of snow, just enough to make things look pretty but not enough as to cause inconvenience.

17 December — holly

> Green groweth the holly,
> So doth the ivy.
> Though winter blasts blow never so high,
> Green groweth the holly.

During winter festivals like the Saturnalia (originally celebrated on 17 December) or Yule (see 21 December), wreaths of holly were brought indoors and displayed to repel evil spirits and to attract good fortune. Henry VIII's carol 'Green Groweth the Holly', published in 1522, emphasizes holly as a symbol of resilience and immortality. For Christians, its bright-red berries and evergreen leaves foretell both the passion of Christ and his resurrection.

18 December

crystalline

Hear the sledges with the bells –
Silver bells!
What a world of merriment their melody foretells!
How they tinkle, tinkle, tinkle,
In the icy air of night!
While the stars that oversprinkle
All the heavens, seem to twinkle
With a crystalline delight;
Keeping time, time, time,
In a sort of Runic rhyme,
To the tintinnabulation that so musically wells
From the bells, bells, bells, bells,
Bells, bells, bells –
From the jingling and the tinkling of the bells.

Edgar Allan Poe, so often haunted by sinister sounds, here begins his poem 'The Bells' by celebrating the crystalline music of winter. Unfortunately, as the poem continues, the merry melody is replaced by tolling and knelling, but here we hear the sharp edges of the tinkling sounds as they roll out in the ice night.

19 December **maujaq**

> One fine winter's day when Piglet was brushing away the snow in front of his house, he happened to look up, and there was Winnie-the-Pooh. Pooh was walking round and round in a circle, thinking of something else, and when Piglet called to him, he just went on walking.
>
> 'Hallo!' said Piglet, 'what are you doing?'...
>
> 'Tracking something,' said Winnie-the-Pooh very mysteriously.
>
> 'Tracking what?' said Piglet, coming closer.
>
> 'That's just what I ask myself. I ask myself, What?... Now, look there.' He pointed to the ground in front of him. 'What do you see there?'

Snow can make it hard to walk, your feet disappearing into deep soft snow that threatens to suck your wellies off your feet. Inuit languages has a word for this kind of snow, of course – *maujaq*.

A A Milne's Winnie-the-Pooh seems to have no trouble snow-walking; his problem is recognizing his own tracks, something in which the Inuit doubtless excel.

20 December **snew**

> If I were a bear, and a big bear too,
> I shouldn't much care if it froze or snew

In Germanic languages, like German and English, a few, so-called 'strong' verbs form their past tenses by changing the root vowel (such as the English blow–blew). Some of these forms like 'snew', found in Middle English, have long since been regularized, so that 'snowed', as the past tense of snow, is now standard (though it clings on in some dialects). What a loss! These lines from A A Milne's children's poem 'Furry Bear' uses 'snew' (as well as 'friz', meaning froze) as whimsical rhymes. How about 'drazzle' or 'rinn' (neologisms both) for other weather past-tense verbs?

21 December

Yule

Yule was the mid-winter festival celebrated among Germanic peoples around the winter solstice and beyond – a week or so of feasting and drinking and generally having fun (much like the modern Christmas, to which its traditions such as 'decking the halls' have contributed). Yule was also more broadly applied to the wintry months of December and January together, sometimes known specifically as *Geol-monaþ* (Yule-month) and *Æftera Geola* (After-Yule).

22 December

hollin

This regional word for holly, from Old English *holen*, is still quite common in Scotland. Holly was an important winter fodder so it survives in lots of place-names such as Thick Hollins (West Yorkshire) and Hollins Green (Cheshire). J R R Tolkien used the name for a lost Elvish kingdom that stood beneath the western flanks of the Misty Mountain, where lots of holly grew. Here he was also drawing on the association of holly with magic and ritual – the Elves of Hollin were the forgers of the Rings of Power.

23 December

snaw-breaker

Not all sheep act sheepish, unwilling to break from the flock. In mid-winter there will be a doughty one who heads off through the deep snow to find food, leaving a channel in her wake. In Scots, she is the snaw-breaker – the rest of the flock will, of course, sheepishly follow.

hush

> To dwellers in a wood almost every species of tree has its voice as well as its feature. At the passing of the breeze the fir-trees sob and moan no less distinctly than they rock; the holly whistles as it battles with itself; the ash hisses amid its quiverings; the beech rustles while its flat boughs rise and fall. And winter, which modifies the note of such trees as shed their leaves, does not destroy its individuality.
>
> On a cold and starry Christmas-eve within living memory a man was passing up a lane towards Mellstock Cross in the darkness of a plantation that whispered thus distinctively to his intelligence. All the evidences of his nature were those afforded by the spirit of his footsteps, which succeeded each other lightly and quickly, and by the liveliness of his voice as he sang in a rural cadence...

The lyrical opening of Thomas Hardy's *Under the Greenwood Tree*, following a group of carol singers as they make their way around a Dorset village, is attentive to the sound of winter, not just its sights – appropriately enough for a book about a parish choir. The sounds of nature may be hushed in winter, especially when the landscape lies under a blanket of deep snow, but really it is a time for us to listen even more carefully – that flutter of wings, that scurry in the undergrowth, that sighing of trees...

25 December — nature

All nature has a feeling: woods, fields, brooks
Are life eternal; and in silence they
Speak happiness beyond the reach of books;
There's nothing mortal in them; their decay
Is the green life of change; to pass away
And come again in blooms revivified.
Its birth was heaven, eternal is its stay,
And with the sun and moon shall still abide
Beneath their day and night and heaven wide.

John Clare's much loved poem 'All Nature has a Feeling' captures some of the quiet calm, silence, and peace we can find in nature. The ineffable feeling created by the passing of the seasons, and the hope of new life in mortality. The word 'nature' evokes new life and birth and has its roots in the Latin verb *nāscī* – to be born – incidentally, the same root as the word nativity.

26 December — hogamadog

If you were lucky enough to have a white Christmas then you may be tempted to build a snowman. In order to start your construction you will need to roll a ball of snow through a snowfield so that it gradually becomes bigger – a hogamadog. This Northumbrian word may be related to a dialect word used for both snail and hedgehog – 'hodmandod' – both rolled up creatures.

27 December — upplega

Another useful Swedish winter word, this one meaning 'uplay' and used to describe the accumulation of snow on the topside of tree branches. The snow thus lying looks very pretty but can damage trees, as the accumulated weight causes branches to snap off. One more reason not to stand under trees!

28 December — niveous

> Wakes from its slumber the suspicious eye,
> And bids it look abroad on hill, and dale,
> Cottage, and steeple, in the niveous stole
> Of Winter trimly dress'd. The silent show'r,
> Precipitated still, no breeze disturbs,
> While fine as dust it falls. Deep on the face
> Of the wide landscape lies the spotless flood
> Accumulating still, a vast expanse,
> Save where the frowning wood without a leaf
> Rears its dark branches on the distant hill.

Niveous means 'of the colour of snow', from the Latin for the stuff, *nix*, as here used by James Hurdis, in his poem 'Favourite Village', about his native Bishopstone, in East Sussex. Use of obscure words for the sake of it is much frowned upon in modern poetry but here strikes a rather lovely note.

29 December

conkerbell

> But a dreadful winter came, longer and more cruel than usual, and sweet little Gwendoline drooped and faded, and Reece had to go alone to the fairies' well, to look for 'conkerbells', as their mother had taught them to call the long icicles that hung from every spray.

This dialect word for icicle – used in Devon, Dorset and Cornwall – was first recorded in the 18th century in a short story in *The Gentleman's Magazine*. The word travelled with settlers from the region to Newfoundland and Labrador, adding to the rich tapestry of the province's language.

30 December

roarie bummler

> My soul is awakened, my spirit is soaring
> And carried aloft on the wings of the breeze;
> For above and around me the wild wind is roaring,
> Arousing to rapture the earth and the seas.
>
> The long withered grass in the sunshine is glancing,
> The bare trees are tossing their branches on high;
> The dead leaves, beneath them, are merrily dancing,
> The white clouds are scudding across the blue sky.
>
> I wish I could see how the ocean is lashing
> The foam of its billows to whirlwinds of spray;
> I wish I could see how its proud waves are dashing,
> And hear the wild roar of their thunder today!

So wrote Anne Brontë on this day in 1842. Like her siblings, Anne embraced wild weather and this poem was inspired by a walk taken in North Yorkshire. The Scots have a word for just the type of white cloud Anne was describing – roarie bummler – evoking the breathless roaring of the sky on a windy day.

gelid

> It is so cold, so very cold – and looks and feels so very much like snow, that if it were to any other place or with any other party, I should really try not to go out to-day – and dissuade my father from venturing; but as he has made up his mind, and does not seem to feel the cold himself, I do not like to interfere, as I know it would be so great a disappointment to Mr and Mrs Weston.

It's New Year's Eve, and we might debate, like Jane Austen's heroine Emma on another cold winter's night, whether it is a good idea to go out to a party, especially when snow is on the ground or in the offing. The Woodhouses and friends do eventually venture out to the Westons' in their carriages and only half an inch of snow falls by the end of the evening, so all, after all, is well.

On the other hand, how much cosier it might be if we stayed in on such a very cold – gelid – night and waited for the New Year quietly and companionably by the fireside?

Happy new year... to you and all of nature.

References

Aitken, Joan. *The Wolves of Willoughby Chase*. Jonathan Cape 1962.
Amundsen, Roald. Report from the *The Mercury*, Hobart, Australia (11 March 1912).
Armitage, Simon. *Dwell*. Faber & Faber, 2025.
Arnold, Matthew, *New Poems*. Macmillan & Co., 1867.
Austen, Jane. *Emma*. John Murray, 1815.
Austen, Jane. *Mansfield Park*. Egerton, 1814.
Austen, Jane. *Northanger Abbey and Persuasion*. John Murray, 1818.
Barker, Cicely Mary. *The Complete Book of the Flower Fairies*. Warne, 2016.
Barnes, William. *Poems of Rural Life in the Dorset Dialect*. Kegan Paul, Trench, Trübner & Co., 1903.
Bashō. Trans. Katie Button.
Belloc, Hilaire. *The Bad Child's Book of Beasts*. The Camelot Press Limited, 1896.
Blake, William. *Songs of Innocence and Experience*. 1794.
Blind, Mathilde. *The Ascent of Man*. Chatto & Windus, 1889.
Bourdillon, Francis William. *Miniscula*. Lawrence & Bullen, 1897.
Breton, Nicholas. *Fantasticks*. Francis Williams, 1626.
Brontë, Ann. *Poems by Currer, Ellis, and Acton Bell*. Aylott and Jones, 1846
Brontë, Charlotte. *Jane Eyre*. Smith, Elder, 1847.
Brontë, Emily. *The Complete Poems*. Penguin, 1992.
Brontë, Emily. *Wuthering Heights*. Thomas Cautley Newby, 1847.
Brooke, Rupert. *The Collected Poems of Rupert Brooke*. The Medici Society, 1919.
Bryant, William Cullen. *Poems*. D Appleton and Company, 1855.
Burns, Robert. *The Poems of Robert Burns and Selected Letters*. Collins, 1959.
Camus, Albert. *The Stranger*. Trans. Stuart Gilbert. Alfred A. Knopf, 1946.
Carr J L. *A Month in the Country*. Harvester Press, 1980.
Carroll, Lewis. *Adventures in Wonderland*. Macmillan & Co., 1865.
Carroll, Lewis. *Through the Looking-Glass*. Macmillan & Co., 1871.
Carter, Angela, 'The Company of Wolves'. In *The Bloody Chamber and Other Stories*. Victor Gollancz, 1979.
Carver, Jonathan. *Travels Through the Interior Parts of North-America, in the Years 1766, 1767, and 1768*. C. Dilly, 1781.
Cawein, Madison Julius. *The Poems of Madison Julius Cawein*. Bobbs-Merrill, 1907.
Chaucer, Geoffrey. *The Canterbury Tales*. Ed. Walter W. Skeat. Clarendon Press, 1894–7.
Clare, John. *Poems*. H. Frowde, 1908.
Coleman, William Stephen. *British Butterflies: Figures and Descriptions of Every Native Species*. George Routledge, 1860.
Coleridge, Samuel Taylor. *The Complete Poetical Works*. Ed. Ernest Hartley Coleridge. Clarendon Press, 1912.
Coleridge, Sarah. *Pretty Lessons in Verse for Good Children*. John W. Parker, 1834.
Coolidge, Susan. *What Katy Did*. Roberts Brothers, 1886.
Cummings, e e. *Tulips and Chimneys*. Thomas Seltzer, 1923.
Dahl, Roald. *My Year*. Heinemann, 1997.
de la Mare, Walter. *Collected Poems, 1901–1918*. H. Holt & Co., 2018.
Dickens, Charles. *Bleak House*. Bradbury & Evans, 1853.
Dickens, Charles. *Great Expectations*. Chapman & Hall, 1861.
Dickens, Charles. *The Pickwick Papers*. Chapman & Hall, 1837
Dickinson, Emily. *Poems by Emily Dickinson, Second Series*. Ed. Mabel Loomis Todd and T W Higginson. *Roberts Brothers*, 1891.

Donne, John. *Selected Poems*. Penguin, 2006.
Dunmore, Helen. *Inside the Wave*. Bloodaxe Books, 2017.
Eliot, George. *The George Eliot Letters*. Yale University Press, 1954.
Eliot, T S, *The Waste Land*. Hogarth Press, 1923.
Emerson, Ralph Waldo. *Poems*. Phillips, Sampson & Company, 1847.
Flanders, Michael, and Swann, Donald. *The Songs of Michael Flanders and Donald Swann*. Faber Music, 2007.
Flaubert, Gustave. *November*. Trans. Andrew Brown. Alma Classics, 2013.
Forster, E M. *A Room with a View*. Edward Arnold, 1908
Freneau, Philip Morin. *The Poems of Philip Freneau*. Ed. Fred Lewis Pattee. The Princeton University library, 1932.
Friel, Brian. *Dancing at Lughnasa*. Faber & Faber, 1990.
Frost, Robert. *Complete Poems*. Henry Holt & Co., 1955.
Galsworthy, John. *The Forsyte Saga*. John Scribner's, 1922.
Galt, John. *The Steam-Boat*. William Blackwood, 1822.
Gawain and the Green Knight. Trans. Simon Amitage. Faber & Faber, 2007.
Gibson, Wilfred Wilson. *Whin*. Macmillan, 2018.
Glück, Louise. *Poems, 1962–2020*. Penguin, 2022.
Gogh, Vincent van. To Theo van Gogh. Arles, Tuesday, 21 or Wednesday, 22 August 1888. The Letters. Ed. Leo Jansen, Hans Luijten and Nienke Bakker. https://vangoghletters.org/vg/letters/let666/letter.html
Goldsmith, Oliver. *The Deserted Village*. W. Griffin, 1770.
Gosse, Edmund. 'The Return of the Swallows'. In *The Collected Poems*. William Heinemann, 1911
Grahame, Kenneth. *The Wind in the Willows*. Methuen & Co., 1908.
Graham, Robert Bontine Cunninghame. *Scottish Stories*, Duckworth & Co., 1914.
Gwilym, Dafydd ap. *Translations into English Verse*. Trans. Arthur James Johnes. Henry Hooper, 1834.
Hale, Sarah Josepha Buell, *Poems for Our Children*. R W Hale, 1916.
Harper, Frances Ellen Watkins. *Poems*. George S Ferguson, 1896.
Hardy, Thomas. *The Complete Poems*. New Wessex Editions, Macmillan, 1976.
Hardy, Thomas. *Far from the Madding Crowd*. Smith, Elder & Co., 1874.
Hardy, Thomas. *Tess of the D'Urbervilles*. James R. Osgood, McIlvaine and Co., 1891.
Hardy, Thomas. *Under the Greenwood Tree*. Holt & Williams, 1872.
Hartley, L P. *The Go-Between*. Hamish Hamilton, 1953.
Hawker, Robert Stephen. In *Footprints of Former Men in Far Cornwall*. John Lane, 1903.
Heaney, Seamus. *The Poems of Seamus Heaney*. Faber & Faber, 2025.
'Here Foloweth Colyn Blowbols Testament'. https://allpoetry.com/Here-Foloweth-Colyn-Blowbols-Testament.
Herrick, Robert. *The Hesperides & Noble Numbers*. Lawrence & Bullen Ltd., 1898
Herriot, James. *All Creatures Great and Small*. St. Martin's Press, 1972.
Higginson, Thomas Wentworth. *Studies in Romance*. Houghton, Mifflin and Company, 1900.
Hood, Thomas. *Whimsicalities, a Periodical Gathering*. Henry Colburn, 1844.
Hopkins, Gerard Manley. *Poems of Gerard Manley Hopkins*. Ed. Robert Bridges. Humphrey Milford, 1918.
Hurdis, James. *The Favourite Village*. Published at the author's own press, 1800.
Ietaka, Fujiwara no. In *A Hundred Verses from Old Japan*, Trans. William N. Porter. Clarendon Press, 1909.
Jacob, Violet. *Songs of Angus*. John Murray, 2015.
Jansson, Tove. *Finn Family Moomintroll*. Trans. Elizabeth Portch. Ernest Benn, 1950.
Jansson, Tove. *Moominland in Midwinter*. Trans. Thomas Warburton. Ernest Benn, 1958.
Jansson, Tove. *Moomin Summer Madness*. Trans. Thomas Warburton. Ernest Benn, 1955.
Jansson, Tove. *The Summer Book*. Trans. Thomas Teal. Pantheon Books, 1974.
Jewett, Sophie. *Persephone and Other Poems.*, Helen J. Sanborn, 1905
Joyce, James. 'The Dead', In *Dubliners*. Grant Richards, 1914.
Kalevala. Trans. John Martin Crawford. Robert Clarke, 1904.

Keats, John. *Selected Poems*. Penguin, 1999.
Keats, John. *Selected Letters*. Penguin, 2014.
Kipling, Rudyard. *The Jungle Book*. Macmillan & Co, 1894
Kiyowara, no Fukayaba. *A Hundred Verses from Old Japan*, Trans. William N. Porter. Clarendon Press, 1909.
Kobayashi, Issa. Trans. Katie Button.
Lawrence, D H. *The Complete Poems*. Ed. Vivian de Sola Pinta and Warren Roberts. Penguin, 1971.
Lawrence, D H. The Rainbow. Methuen & Co, 1915.
Lear, Edward. *Nonsense Songs, Stories, Botany, and Alphabets*. Robert John Bush, 1871.
Lee, Laurie, *Cider with Rosie*. Hogarth, 1959.
Lewis, C S. *The Lion, the Witch and the Wardrobe*. Geoffrey Bles, 1950.
Lindsay, Nicholas Vachel. *General William Booth enters into Heaven, and other poems*. The Macmillan Company 1916.
Longfellow, Henry Wadsworth. *The Song of Hiawatha*. Ticknor and Fields, 1885.
Lowell, Amy. *A Dome of Many-Coloured Glass*. Houghton Mifflin Company. 1912.
Lowell, Amy. *Pictures of a Floating World*. Houghton Mifflin Company. 1919.
Marlowe, Christopher. *The Complete Poems and Translations*. Ed. Stephen Orgel. Penguin, 1971.
Martin, George R R. *A Game of Thrones*. HarperCollins Voyager, 1996.
Marvell, Andrew. *The Complete Poems*. Penguin, 1976.
Masefield, John. *Selected Poems*. William Heinemann, 1922.
MacDonald, George. *Works of Fancy and Imagination*. Strahan and Co., 1871.
McClellan, George Marion. *The Book of American Negro Poetry*. Harcourt, Brace and Company, 1922.
McCrae, John. 'In Flanders Fields'. In *Punch*, 8 December 1915.
Milne, A A. *Now We Are Six*. E P Dutton & Co., 1927.
Milne, A A. *Winnie-the-Pooh*. Methuen & Co., 1926.
Mitsune, Ōshikōchi no. *A Hundred Verses from Old Japan*, Trans. William N. Porter. Clarendon Press, 1909.
Montale, Eugenio. 'Meriggiare pallido e assorto'. In *Ossi di seppia* [Cuttlefish Bones]. Piero Gobetti Editori, 1925.
Morris, William , 'Pomona'. William Morris Archive, accessed April 10, 2026, https://morris-archive.lib.uiowa.edu/items/show/2283.
Morris, William, 'The Orchard'. William Morris Archive, accessed April 10, 2026, https://morrisarchive.lib.uiowa.edu/items/show/2285.
Morris, William, 'The Woodpecker'. William Morris Archive, accessed April 10, 2026, https://morrisarchive.lib.uiowa.edu/items/show/2280.
Murdoch, Iris. *The Sea, the Sea*. Chatto & Windus, 1978.
'Old English Rune Poem'. Trans. Bruce Dickins. In *Runic and heroic poems of the old Teutonic peoples*. Cambridge University Press, 1915.
Nairn, Lady. *The Book of Scottish Song*. Blackie and Son, 1843
Picken, Ebenezer. *Poems and Epistles, mostly in the Scottish dialect*. Reprint edition. British Library, 2011.
Plath, Sylvia. 'Faun'. In *The Colossus and Other Poems*. William Heinemann, 1960.
Plath, Sylvia. *Fiesta Melons*. Rougemont Press, 1971.
Pliny the Elder. *The Natural History*. Trans. Harris Rackham. Loeb Classical Library., 1942.
Potter, Beatrix. *The Tale of Squirrel Nutkin*. Frederick Warne & Co., 1903.
Powys, John Cowper. *A Glastonbury Romance*. Simon & Schuster, 1932.
Pratchett, Terry. *The Wee Free Men*. Doubleday, 2003.
Proust, Marcel. *Swann's Way*. Trans. Charles Kennet Scott Montcrieff. Henry Holt & Co. 1922.
Pullman, Philip. *Northern Lights*. Scholastic, 1995.
Ramsay, Allan. *The Gentle Shepherd: A Pastoral Comedy*. William Gowans, 1852.
Rorie, David. *The Auld Doctor and other Poems and Songs in Scots*. Constable & Company Ltd. 1920.
Rossetti, Christina. *Goblin Market, The Prince's Progress and Other Poems*. Macmillan, 1875.
Rossetti, Dante Gabriel. *Poems and Translations 1850–1870*. Oxford University Press, 1913.

Sadayori, Fujiwara no. In *A Hundred Verses from Old Japan*, Trans. William N. Porter. Clarendon Press, 1909
Saigyō Hōshi, Trans. Katie Button.
Sappho, 'Midnight' song. Trans. J. A. Symonds. in *The Poems of Sappho*. Williams and Norgate, 1924.
Setoun, Gabriel. *The Child World*. John Lane the Bodley Head, 1896.
Shakespeare, William. *The Oxford Shakespeare: The Complete Works*, 2nd edn. Ed. Stanley Wells and Gary Taylor. Oxford University Press, 2005.
Shelley, Percy Bysse. *Prometheus Unbound*. C. and J. Ollier, 1820.
Shepherd, Nan. *The Sacred Mountain*. Canongate Books, 2011.
Shiki, Masaoka. Trans Katie Button.
Simpson, Margaret Winefride. https://www.scotslanguage.com/poetry?calendar=Apr_2011
Smith, Maggie, 'Starlings'. *The Southern Review*, Summer 2018.
Sorley, Charles Hamilton. *Marlborough and Other Poems*. Cambridge University Press, 1916.
Stevenson, Robert Louis. 'Autumn Fires'. In *A Child's Garden of Verses.* Charles Scribner's Sons, 1905.
Stevenson, Robert Louis. 'Winter-Time'. In *A Child's Garden of Verses.* Charles Scribner's Sons, 1905.
Stoddard, Elizabeth. 'The Willow Boughs are Yellow Now' In *Poems*. Houghton, Mifflin and Company, 1895.
Stoker, Bram. *Dracula*. Archibald Constable and Company, 1897.
Tagore, Rabindranath. In *The English Writings*. Sahitya Akademi, 1994.
Tennyson, Lord Alfred. *Idylls of the King*. Edward Moxon, 1859.
Tennyson, Lord Alfred. *Two Voices*. *In Poems*. Edward Moxon, 1842.
Thomas, Edward. *Poems*. Selwyn & Blount, 1917.
Thomas, Dylan. *Collected Poems, 1934–1952*. J M Dent, 1952.
Tolkien, J R R. *The Adventures of Tom Bombadil*. George Allen & Unwin, 1962.
Tolkien, J R R. *The Hobbit*. George Allen & Unwin, 1937.
Tolkien, J R R. 'The King's Letter' (Marquette MS Tolkien 3/9/35 1r), published in Vinyar Tengwar 29 (May 1993), cover.
Tolkien, J R R. *The Fellowship of the Ring*. George Allen & Unwin, 1954.
Tolkien, J R R. *The Two Towers*. George Allen & Unwin, 1954.
Turgenev, Ivan. *Turgenev's Letters*. Ed. A. V. Knowles. Bloomsbury Academic, 1983.
Twain, Mark. *Tom Sawyer, Detective*. Harper & Brothers, 1896.
Twain, Mark (after Robert Richardson). 'Warm Summer Sun'. Epitaph for Olivia Susan Clemens, Woodlawn Cemetery, Elmira, New York.
Tynan, Katherine. *Twenty One Poems*. Dun Emer Press, 1907.
Verlaine, Paul. 'L'Heure exquise'. In *La Bonne Chanson*. Alphonse Lemerre, 1870. Trans. Robert Tuesley Anderson.
'The Whale'. In *The Old English Physiologus*. Trans. James Hall Pitman. Yale University Press and Oxford University Press, 1821.
Whitman, Walt. *Specimen Days*. Rees Welsh and Company, 1882.
Wilde, Jane. *Ancient Legends, Mystic Charms & Superstitions of Ireland*. Chatto & Windus, 1919.
Wilder, Laura Ingalls. *Little House in the Big Woods*. Harper & Brothers, 1932.
William, William Carlos. *Sour Grapes*. The Four Seasons Company, 1921.
William, William Carlos. *Spring and All*, Contact Publishing Co., 1923.
Woolf, Virginia. *Correspondence, 1882–1941*. The Hogarth Press, 1975.
Woolf, Virginia. *Orlando*. The Hogarth Press, 1928.
Woolf, Virginia. *The Waves*. The Hogarth Press, 1931.
Wordsworth, Dorothy. *Journals*. Ed. William Knight. Macmillan, 1897.
Wordsworth, William. *The Collected Poems*. Wordsworth Editions, 1994.
Virgil, *The Georgics*, Trans. John Dryden. In *The Works of John Dryden*, William Miller, 1808.
Whittier, John Greenleaf. *The Works of John Greenleaf Whittier*. Houghton Mifflin, 1892.
Yeats, William Butler. The Countess Kathleen and Various Legends and Lyrics. T. Fisher Unwin, 1892.

Dear Reader,

We'd love your attention for one more page to tell you about the crisis in children's reading, and what we can all do.

Studies have shown that reading for fun is the **single biggest predictor of a child's future life chances** – more than family circumstance, parents' educational background or income. It improves academic results, mental health, wealth, communication skills, ambition and happiness.[1]

The number of children reading for fun is in rapid decline. Young people have a lot of competition for their time. In 2024, 1 in 10 children and young people in the UK aged 5 to 18 did not own a single book at home.[2]

Hachette works extensively with schools, libraries and literacy charities, but here are some ways we can all raise more readers:

- Reading to children for just 10 minutes a day makes a difference
- Don't give up if children aren't regular readers – there will be books for them!
- Visit bookshops and libraries to get recommendations
- Encourage them to listen to audiobooks
- Support school libraries
- Give books as gifts

There's a lot more information about how to encourage children to read on our website: **www.RaisingReaders.co.uk**

Thank you for reading.

---

[1] OECD, '21st-Century Readers: Developing Literacy Skills in a Digital World', 2021, https://www.oecd.org/en/publications/21st-century-readers_a83d84cb-en.html

[2] National Literacy Trust, 'Book Ownership in 2024'. November 2024, https://literacytrust.org.uk/research-services/research-reports/book-ownership-in-2024